Deepening Insight

Teachings on *vedanā* in the
Early Buddhist Discourses

D1553880

Bhikkhu Anālayo

PARIYATTI PRESS
an imprint of
Pariyatti Publishing
www.pariyatti.org

ISBN: 978-1-68172-403-4 (Print)
ISBN: 978-1-68172-404-1 (PDF)
ISBN: 978-1-68172-405-8 (ePub)
ISBN: 978-1-68172-406-5 (Mobi)
Library of Congress Control Number: 2021940450

As an act of *Dhammadāna*, Bhikkhu Anālayo has waived royalty payments for this book.

Cover photo by Inge Maria on Unsplash
(https://unsplash.com/photos/pv2ZlDfstXc)

A [true] master of knowledge
Has passed beyond all that is known
And become dispassionate toward all *vedanās*.

(Sn 529)

DEDICATION

This book is dedicated to the
memory of S. N. Goenka
(1924 to 2013).

Acknowledgement

The author happily acknowledges his indebtedness to Chris Burke, Bhikkhunī Dhammadinnā, Linda Grace, Yuka Nakamura, Michael Running, and Bhikṣuṇī Syinchen for commenting on a draft version of this book and to the staff, board members, and supporters of the Barre Center for Buddhist Studies for providing him with the living conditions required to write and meditate.

CONTENTS

INTRODUCTION

The ensuing pages present a selection of passages from the early Buddhist discourses that provide perspectives on the cultivation of liberating insight into *vedanā*, "sensation," "feeling," or "feeling tone." For meditators, such passages can be of considerable help as a reference point for deepening insight.

My presentation is based on textual sources that reflect "early Buddhism," which stands for the development of thought and practices during roughly the first two centuries in the history of Buddhism, from about the fifth to the third century BCE. These sources are the Pāli discourses and their parallels, mostly extant in Chinese translation, which go back to instructions and teachings given orally by the Buddha and his disciples. In those times in India, writing was not employed for such purposes, and for centuries these teachings were transmitted orally. The final results of such oral transmission are available to us nowadays in the form of written texts.

Due to the vagaries of oral transmission, an appreciation of the "early Buddhist" perspective on a particular teaching, in the sense of bringing us as close as possible to the time when the Buddha lived, can greatly benefit from taking into account parallel versions of a particular discourse or passage, as such comparison can help detect errors that occurred during transmission. My presentation is meant to provide direct access, through the medium of translation, to the Chinese *Āgama* parallels to relevant Pāli discourses. The extracts translated below come together with a reference to the relevant page in the standard translation of the respective Pāli version, so that interested readers can do their own comparison beyond the few points of interest that I have mentioned. In order to facilitate comparison, in my translation I adopt Pāli terminology, even though the original used for translation into Chinese was not in Pāli.

I begin my exploration with passages from the *Saṃyukta-āgama*, a collection that is particularly rich in material relevant to an understanding of *vedanā*, followed by taking up the other three Chinese discourse collections. The texts surveyed in this way, which follow the sequence in which they occur in these collections, throw into relief the remarkable potential of contemplating *vedanā* as a powerful avenue for progress to awakening. In commenting on such passages, my chief concern throughout is to bring out practical aspects that are relevant to actual insight meditation.

May this little collection serve as a support for those who have sincerely embarked on the path to liberation.

WATER BUBBLES

The early discourses illustrate the nature of *vedanā* with a wealth of similes and metaphors. These can be of considerable support to meditation practice, as they can capture deep insight themes in a way that is intuitive and does not require much conceptual input. Several of these similes and metaphors occur in the *Saṃyukta-āgama*, a collection of shorter discourses assembled topic wise extant in Chinese, which has its counterpart in the Pāli *Saṃyutta-nikāya*. Out of the four Chinese *Āgamas*, the *Saṃyukta-āgama* is the collection that has the majority of textual material relevant to *vedanā*.[1] The same holds for its Pāli counterpart, the *Saṃyutta-nikāya*, which also has considerably more material on *vedanā* than the other Pāli *Nikāyas*.

My survey of relevant material from the *Saṃyukta-āgama* collection begins with a particularly powerful metaphor to illustrate the nature of *vedanā*: bubbles on a water surface during rain. This image occurs in the context of a series of analogies for each of the five aggregates (Pāli parallel: SN 22.95). For the second aggregate of *vedanā*, the relevant passage in the *Saṃyukta-āgama* proceeds as follows:[2]

> Monastics, it is just as when during a great rain there are bubbles on [the surface of] water,[3] arising and ceasing one after another, and clear-sighted persons carefully examine, attend to, and analyze them. When carefully examining, attending to, and analyzing them, [they find that] there is nothing in them, nothing stable, nothing substantial; they have no solidity. Why is that? It is because there is nothing solid or substantial in water bubbles.

In the same way, monastics carefully examine, attend to, and analyze any *vedanā*, past, future, or present, internal or external, gross or subtle, sublime or repugnant, far or near. When carefully examining, attending to, and analyzing them, the monastics [find that] there is nothing in them, nothing stable, nothing substantial; they have no solidity. They are like a disease, like a carbuncle, like a thorn, like a killer; they are impermanent, *dukkha*, empty, and not self.[4] Why is that? It is because there is nothing solid or substantial in *vedanā*s.

A central implication of this illustration is the ephemeral and insubstantial nature of *vedanā*s. Just as a bubble can for a moment take up quite a bit of space but will soon vanish completely, so *vedanā*s can have a rather strong impact, especially in the case of intense happiness or pain. Yet, they are ultimately as insubstantial as bubbles, bound to burst soon enough and disappear completely, leaving nothing behind.

Just as a bubble results from the contact of raindrops with the water on the surface of a lake or pond, in the same way, a *vedanā* just results from contact between a sense organ and the corresponding consciousness. This understanding further drives home the actual insubstantiality of *vedanā*s, however substantial they may appear subjectively.

In this way, the image of the bubble can be employed to represent a combination of the central teachings on impermanence and insubstantiality in a way that is directly related to the case of *vedanā*s. The main import of the present passage can be applied in meditation practice or even in daily life in a way that does not require the aid of much conceptual input, by simply arousing the mental image of a bubble about to burst. This image can serve as a succinct reminder of the true nature of *vedanā*s and offer support in remaining balanced and unshaken in the face of any *vedanā* that may be bubbling up.

THE SIX SENSES

A more detailed examination of the relationship between *vedanā* and the six senses, together with a highlight on the inappropriateness of considering *vedanā* to be a self, can be found in the *Chachakka-sutta* (MN 148) and its parallels. The discourse begins by delineating various types of "sixes," such as the six senses, their corresponding objects, the respective type of contact, until it eventually comes to the six types of *vedanā*. The latter receives the following definition in the *Saṃyukta-āgama* parallel:[5]

> What are the six types of *vedanā*? That is, they are *vedanā* arisen from eye-contact, *vedanā* arisen from ear-contact, *vedanā* arisen from nose-contact, *vedanā* arisen from tongue-contact, *vedanā* arisen from body-contact, and *vedanā* arisen from mind-contact.

Compared to the above extract, the *Chachakka-sutta* presents a more detailed account of the dependent arising of *vedanā* in relation to each of the six senses. For the case of the eye, for example, the *Chachakka-sutta* points out that eye-consciousness arises in dependence on eye and form, the conjunction of the three being contact, which in turn forms the condition for *vedanā*.

In both versions, the pointer to the conditioned nature of the six types of *vedanā*, whether given succinctly or in detail, leads on to an understanding of the nature of *vedanā* as not self. This takes the following form in the *Saṃyukta-āgama* discourse:[6]

> It is thus not the case that *vedanā* arisen from eye-contact could be a self. Why is that? [It is because]

vedanā arisen from eye-contact is of a nature to arise and cease. If *vedanā* arisen from eye-contact were a self, then the self would in turn undergo birth and death [each time a *vedanā* arises or ceases]. For this reason, it is thus not the case that one could proclaim *vedanā* arisen from eye-contact to be a self. For this reason, *vedanā* arisen from eye-contact is not self.

In agreement with its Pāli parallel, the *Saṃyukta-āgama* discourse applies the same reasoning to the other senses. From a practical perspective, this presentation provides an easily accessible avenue for arousing insight into not self. Whatever sense door is taken up for contemplation, the *vedanās* experienced are invariably of an impermanent nature (as are the respective object, consciousness, and contact involved). By applying the analysis into six distinct senses in this way to the experience of *vedanā*, it becomes unmistakably clear that any experience is but a changing process, leaving no room to posit some unchanging and eternal entity anywhere.

WHO FEELS?

The topic of not self comes up right away again in the next passage to be taken up (Pāli parallel: SN 12.12), which reports the Buddha replying to the question: "Who feels?" The *Saṃyukta-āgama* version proceeds in this way:[7]

> I do not say that there is 'one who feels.' If I were to say that there is 'one who feels,' you could ask: 'Who feels?'

> You should [instead] ask: 'Because of what conditions is there *vedanā*?' I would answer in this way: 'In dependence on contact there is *vedanā*.'

Bhikkhu Bodhi (2000: 732n22) explains that the corresponding question "Who feels?" in the Pāli version "is 'pregnant' with an implicit view of self ... The Buddha must therefore reject as invalid the question itself, which is based on an illegitimate assumption." In other words, the question "Who feels?" is rejected because it comes with the underlying assumption that the reply will assert some kind of substantial entity that stands in the background of the experience of *vedanā*.

For further clarification, the position that emerges in this way could be related to a recommendation in the Pāli commentary on the *Satipaṭṭhāna-sutta* that involves the same type of question: "Who feels?"[8] The commentary continues by right away providing the answer that there is no substantial being or person who feels. According to the commentary, this understanding marks the crucial difference between merely being aware of *vedanās* and their contemplation as an establishment of mindfulness (*satipaṭṭhāna*).

The perspective provided in the commentary concords with the impression that the problem in the above discourse passage was the underlying assumption by the questioner, who was thinking in terms of substantial reified essences instead of viewing the matter in terms of conditionality. With this clarification in mind, the present discourse can be taken as an invitation to step out of thinking (and perceiving) in substantialized ways and instead shift to seeing just processes that are the result of causes and conditions.

For such a shift of perspective, it can be helpful if a foundation is laid by recognizing the sense of self-referentiality that tends to lurk at the background of unawakened experience.

Mindfulness can be directed inward, with a sense of curiosity and investigation, in order to discern that the construction of a self simply lacks any foundation.

Dependence on Contact

With the next discourse my exploration of passages relevant to *vedanā* proceeds to the collection of discourses specifically assembled under this topic, whose Pāli counterpart is the *Vedanā-saṃyutta*, the "collected discourses on *vedanā*."[9] The first discourse in the section of the *Saṃyukta-āgama* dedicated to the topic of *vedanā* turns right away to the key question in relation to *vedanā*: the need to cultivate insight into its conditioned nature:[10]

> There are three *vedanā*s: unpleasant *vedanā*, pleasant *vedanā*, and neutral *vedanā*. What is the condition for these three *vedanā*s, how do they arise, how do they grow, how do they evolve? That is, these three *vedanā*s are conditioned by contact, they arise from contact, they grow from contact, and they evolve from contact. Conditioned by a particular contact, a particular *vedanā* arises. If that particular contact ceases, that particular *vedanā* also ceases, ends, becomes cool, and disappears.
>
> Knowing like this and seeing like this in relation to this [body] of mine with consciousness, external objects, and any signs, one gains the vision that there is no self or what belongs to a self [as a basis for] the underlying tendency, fetter, and attachment toward the I-conceit.

The Pāli version (SN 36.10) presents the same basic dependency of *vedanā* on contact by taking up each of its three types individually for treatment, followed by illustrating the situation with the example of the production of fire, which in the ancient Indian setting depended on the rubbing together of fire sticks.[11] Although more detailed in this respect, the *Saṃyutta-nikāya* parallel does not describe how the resultant knowledge and vision lead on to insight into not self.

Common to the two parallels is thus the dependence of the affective tone of *vedanā* on the type of contact that causes its arising. A particular contact will lead to the corresponding *vedanā*. This clarification in a way directs attention away from attempts to change *vedanā* itself, a common but misguided attempt. Instead, wise directing of attention to the absence of a self can make a world of difference when actually experiencing the three types of *vedanā*.

On experiencing the first impact of these three types of *vedanā*, there is a possibility to choose how attention will be directed. Rather than letting attention just stay with the particular *vedanā*, vainly hoping that it will stay (if pleasant) or disappear (if unpleasant), attention can turn inward to discern the empty nature of any experience of *vedanā*.

THREE PERCEPTIONS

The next discourse provides what can be considered a complementary perspective on the previous one: How should each of the three types of *vedanā* be regarded? The relevant passage clarifies this in the following manner:[12]

> There are three *vedanās*: unpleasant *vedanā*, pleasant *vedanā*, and neutral *vedanā*. Contemplate pleasant *vedanā* by perceiving it as unsatisfactory (*dukkha*). Contemplate unpleasant *vedanā* by perceiving it as the tip of a sword. Contemplate neutral *vedanā* by perceiving it as impermanent [and bound to cease]. If a monastic contemplates pleasant *vedanā* by perceiving it as unsatisfactory, contemplates unpleasant *vedanā* by perceiving it as the tip of a sword, and contemplates neutral *vedanā* by perceiving it as impermanent and [bound to] cease, this is called right view.

The Pāli parallel (SN 36.5) continues by pointing out that one who rightly sees in this way has cut off craving, severed the fetters, comprehended conceit, and made an end of *dukkha*. Both versions continue with verses, which in the Chinese version also contain expressions reflecting the attainment of the final goal. In this way, the two versions agree on the liberating potential of contemplating *vedanā* in the manner described above.

The implication of the individual recommendations made in each case can best be explored in relation to the next discourse, which takes up the three *vedanās* from the viewpoint of their respective underlying tendencies.

Of further significance in the present discourse is the indication that such contemplation of *vedanās* serves as right view, the first factor in the noble eightfold path.

For the unfolding of this path, right view is of central importance by providing the appropriate sense of direction that serves to align the other path factors. This endows the above presentation with considerable significance, since it enables a practical approach to right view that is directly related to *vedanā*.

According to a recurrent definition found elsewhere in the discourses, right view can take the form of insight into the four noble truths. The present exposition could in fact be considered a specific adaptation of such right view so as to be directly relevant to the particular case of *vedanā*. Needless to say, for someone dedicated to contemplation of *vedanā*s, the four noble truths form an ideal framework for meditation practice and daily life. In addition to the provision of such a framework, however, the present discourse could be taken to spell how to apply this by appropriately facing each of the three types of *vedanā*. Such facing can then serve as the guiding principle of right view for cultivating the other seven factors of the path.

The Underlying Tendencies

The theme of how each type of *vedanā* should be contemplated stands in close relationship to the underlying tendencies (*anusaya*). The discourses often mention a set of seven such underlying tendencies, three of which are of particular relevance to contemplating *vedanās*. In the Pāli discourses, these are the underlying tendencies to passion (*rāga*), aversion (*paṭigha*), and ignorance (*avijjā*). A passage that spells out the matter in detail is part of an instruction given by the Buddha to his son Rāhula. The relevant part proceeds in this way:[13]

> There are three *vedanās*: unpleasant *vedanā*, pleasant *vedanā*, and neutral *vedanā*.[14] One cultivates the holy life under me [i.e., the Buddha] for the sake of abandoning the underlying tendency to passion in relation to pleasant *vedanā*. One cultivates the holy life under me for the sake of abandoning the underlying tendency to aversion in relation to unpleasant *vedanā*. One cultivates the holy life under me for the sake of abandoning the underlying tendency to ignorance in relation to neutral *vedanā*.
>
> Rāhula, if monastics already know they have abandoned the underlying tendency to passion in relation to pleasant *vedanā*, already know they have abandoned the underlying tendency to aversion in relation to unpleasant *vedanā*, already know they have abandoned the underlying tendency to ignorance in relation to neutral *vedanā*, then such monastics are reckoned to have abandoned the bondage of craving and desire, left behind all fetters, and by fully comprehending conceit have completely made an end of *dukkha*.

In agreement with its Pāli parallel (SN 36.3), the above discourse continues by repeating the main teaching in verse form.[15] This main teaching can be summarized as follows:

pleasant *vedanā*:	tendency to passion
unpleasant *vedanā*:	tendency to aversion
neutral *vedanā*:	tendency to ignorance

This serves to flesh out the basic relationship which in the standard presentation of dependent arising (to be explored below p. 52) obtains between *vedanā* and craving. The analysis of *vedanā* into three types allows identifying more clearly the respective types of reaction. Pleasant *vedanā* tends to fuel craving for more. Unpleasant *vedanā* tends to result in craving for its absence, expressed through irritation and aversion. Neutral *vedanā* tends to trigger craving for something more entertaining as an escape from the blandness of experience, an attempt to ignore neutral *vedanā* which thereby succumbs to the modality of ignorance.

The correlation of the three types of *vedanā* to the three underlying tendencies can in turn be combined with the advice given in the preceding discourse. Based on such correlation, it becomes clear that pleasant *vedanā* should be seen as unsatisfactory to counter the tendency to passion. Taking up next the case of neutral *vedanā*, this should be seen as impermanent to counter the tendency to ignorance (both in the sense of disregarding its existence and in the sense of not understanding the true nature of *vedanā*). These two recommendations are quite straightforward.

The case still to be covered is unpleasant or painful *vedanā*, which should be seen as the tip of a sword (or a dart, according to the Pāli version). The task here is to counter the tendency to aversion. Keeping this task in mind helps flesh out the significance of the comparison with the tip of a sword or a dart. The need to avoid aversion makes it clear that the idea is not to encourage emphasizing the afflictive dimension of the experience of this type of *vedanā*, as the comparison with the tip of a sword or a dart could seem to suggest. Instead, these similes need to be employed in such a way that the resultant form of practice leads to a decrease of the tendency to become irritated and aversive.

The significance of these similes will become clearer with the discourse after the next one, which presents the simile of the dart to explain how to face pain. Before coming to that explanation, however, the next discourse puts a highlight on the way pain can impact the mind, thereby further fleshing out the degree to which unpleasant *vedanā*s can overwhelm the mind with their tendency to stimulate aversion.

THE ABYSS OF PAIN

The experience of pain can at times be overwhelming, comparable to an abyss. Yet, with meditative training it becomes possible to avoid falling into this abyss. The two basic responses, when facing this abyss of pain, find expression in the following way:[16]

> The abysmal great ocean is what foolish people in the world call an abyss, which is not what is called an abyss in the noble teaching and discipline. What is called such in the world is just a great accumulation of water. If one is oppressed by *vedanā*s of manifold pains that arise from the body, which torment or kill, this is called being in the place of an extreme abyss.[17]
>
> Being oppressed by painful *vedanā*s arisen in this body, which torment or kill, foolish unlearned worldlings sorrow, lament, cry, and wail; their minds [give rise] to confusion and derangement. They sink for a long time, without a place of rest.
>
> Being oppressed by painful *vedanā*s arisen in this body, which torment or kill, learned noble disciples do not give rise to sorrow, [lamentation], crying, and wailing; their minds do [not] give rise to confusion and derangement. They do not sink in birth and death, having gained a place of rest.

The Pāli version (SN 36.4) makes the same basic contrast in terms of either not rising up from the abyss or rising up from it, having gained a foothold. The two parallels repeat the basic message in verse, which highlights the need to endure pain with patience.[18] Patient endurance would indeed offer a place of rest or a foothold that helps to avoid sinking in the abyss of pain.

This can be related to the implication of the image discussed above, which recommended the perception of pain as the tip of a sword or a dart. The recommendation is to find a place of rest or a foothold by developing the appropriate mental response to bodily pain, so that the underlying tendency to aversion does not get triggered. Such would indeed be possible through cultivating patient endurance. How to go about this receives further elaboration with the image of a dart in the next discourse.

THE DART

The present discourse offers a particularly powerful illustration of how to face the abyss of pain, by way of illustrating its nature with the example of being shot by a dart or arrow:[19]

> To foolish unlearned worldlings through bodily contact *vedanās* arise that are increasingly painful, even leading to the ending of life. They are worried and complain by crying and wailing; their minds give rise to confusion and derangement. At that time two *vedanās* increase, bodily *vedanā* and mental *vedanā*.
>
> It is just like a person whose body has been afflicted by two poisonous arrows and extremely painful *vedanās* arise. Foolish unlearned worldlings are also just like this, increasing two *vedanās*, bodily *vedanā* and mental *vedanā*, [when] extremely painful *vedanās* arise. Why is that? It is because those foolish unlearned worldlings lack understanding.
>
> Being contacted by pleasant *vedanā* arisen from the five [strands of] sensuality, they cling to the pleasure of the five [strands of] sensuality. Because of clinging to the pleasure of the five [strands of] sensuality, they are affected by the underlying tendency to passion.
>
> Because of being contacted by painful *vedanā*, they then give rise to aversion. Because of giving rise to aversion, they are affected by the underlying tendency to aversion.
>
> In relation to these two *vedanās*, they do not understand as it really is their arising, their cessation, their gratification, their disadvantage, and the release from them. Because of not understanding them as they

really are, when neutral *vedanā* arises, they are affected by the underlying tendency to ignorance.

They are bound by pleasant *vedanā*, not freed from it, bound by unpleasant *vedanā*, not freed from it, and bound by neutral *vedanā*, not freed from it. By what are they bound? That is, they are bound by passion, aversion, and ignorance, and bound by birth, old age, disease, death, worry, sorrow, vexation, and pain.

To learned noble disciples through bodily contact painful *vedanā* arises that is greatly painful and oppressive, even leading to the ending of life. They do not give rise to worry or complain by crying and wailing, and their mind does not [give rise] to confusion or derangement. At that time only one *vedanā* arises, namely bodily *vedanā*; mental *vedanā* does not arise.

It is just like a person who is afflicted by one poisonous arrow and not afflicted by a second poisonous arrow. [For learned noble disciples] at that time only one *vedanā* arises, namely bodily *vedanā*; mental *vedanā* does not arise.

Being contacted by pleasant *vedanā*, they are not defiled by the pleasure of sensuality. Because of not being defiled by the pleasure of sensuality, in relation to pleasant *vedanā* they are not affected by the underlying tendency to passion.

Being contacted by unpleasant *vedanā*, they do not give rise to aversion. Because of not giving rise to aversion, they are not affected by the underlying tendency to aversion.

In relation to these two *vedanā*s,[20] they understand as it really is their arising, their cessation, their gratification,[21] their disadvantage, and the release from them. Because of understanding them as they really are, with neutral *vedanā* they are not affected by the underlying tendency to ignorance.

They are liberated from pleasant *vedanā*, not bound by it, liberated from unpleasant *vedanā* and from neutral *vedanā*, not bound by them. By what are they not bound? That is, they are not bound by passion, aversion, and ignorance, and not bound by birth, old age, disease, death, worry, sorrow, vexation, and pain."[22]

In the Pāli version (SN 36.6), the arrows or darts are not poisoned.[23] This offers a more meaningful presentation. With a poisonous arrow the main problem of being poisoned arises already on being hit by a single arrow. A real difference only manifests when the question at stake is just the pain of being hurt by one or two arrows. This is what the simile is meant to illustrate, namely that the first arrow of physical pain need not lead on to the second arrow caused by mental reaction to the pain.

Another difference is that the *Saṃyutta-nikāya* discourse offers an additional explanation of the predicament of worldlings who seek sensual pleasure when being afflicted by pain. They do so because they do not know another alternative to the experience of pain.[24] This helps to link the exposition of pain to the ensuing discussion of pleasant *vedanā*, an interrelation that is not as evident in the version translated above.

Being confronted by pain, the response of the untrained mind is to want to get away from it as soon as possible. Sensual indulgence offers the vain promise of providing an escape from the pain; hence the untrained mind reacts to pain by chasing after sensual pleasure (perhaps even more than anyway done ordinarily). As the discourse clarifies, the net result is to increase the bondage to *vedanā* ever more.

The situation differs substantially when the mind has been trained. The crucial difference is that the arrow of physical pain need not lead on to the additional arrow of mental sorrow. Once mental training makes it possible to experience only the bodily *vedanā* of pain but not the mental one, aversion no longer manifests and the automatic response of searching for sensual indulgence also does not get triggered. The reason is the clear understanding that there is an alternative to handling painful *vedanā* other than sensual indulgence. This alternative is to face the challenge of pain with a balanced mind, rather than react to it with an unbalanced mind.

This, then, is the implication of seeing unpleasant *vedanā* as the tip of a sword or a dart. The task is to avoid increasing the pain that is already there from being struck by the tip of a sword or hit by a dart. Such avoidance requires training oneself in the right mental attitude, inculcating the type of inner balance that is able to react to the impact of pain with mindfulness and patience.

WINDS IN THE SKY

The image that compares *vedanās* to bubbles, which could be employed to implement the instructions in the previous discourse, is not the only metaphor the discourses present to illustrate the nature of *vedanā*. Another passage, which also relates to the cultivation of mental balance when faced with *vedanā*, presents an exemplification of their nature based on the idea of winds in the sky:[25]

> It is just as fierce winds that can suddenly arise in the sky, coming from the four directions: winds that are dusty or winds that are not dusty, all-pervading winds or all-destroying winds, weak winds or strong winds, even whirlwinds.
>
> The 'winds' of *vedanās* in the body are also just like that. Various types of *vedanās* arise one after the other: pleasant *vedanās*, unpleasant *vedanās*, and neutral *vedanās*;
>
> pleasant bodily *vedanās*, unpleasant bodily *vedanās*, and neutral bodily *vedanās*; pleasant mental *vedanās*, unpleasant mental *vedanās*, and neutral mental *vedanās*;
>
> worldly pleasant *vedanās*, worldly unpleasant *vedanās*, worldly neutral *vedanās*; unworldly pleasant, unworldly unpleasant, and unworldly neutral *vedanās*;
>
> pleasant *vedanās* [related to] passion, unpleasant *vedanās* [related to] passion, and neutral *vedanās* [related to] passion; pleasant *vedanās* [related to] renunciation, unpleasant *vedanās* [related to] renunciation, and neutral *vedanās* [related to] renunciation.

The *Saṃyutta-nikāya* parallel (SN 36.12) only mentions the basic distinction into three types of *vedanās* according to their affective tone as pleasant, unpleasant, or neutral, and does not provide a further distinction into different types. The Pāli simile illustrating the nature of *vedanā* additionally mentions cold and hot winds; it does not refer to all-pervading and all-destroying winds or to whirlwinds. Both discourses continue with a set of verses illustrating the basic teaching.[26]

The image of different winds in the sky can conveniently be related to the vicissitudes of the weather. Although there is a fairly widespread tendency among people to complain about the ups and downs of the weather, on proper reflection this turns out to be meaningless and simply a waste of one's time and energy. The same holds for complaining about the ups and downs of *vedanā*.

Instead of getting upset, we simply take hold of an umbrella or whatever other protective equipment may be appropriate to face the weather that has manifested in the best way possible. Similarly, taking hold of the inner protective equipment possible through mindfulness practice, we are ready to face *vedanā* in whatever way it may manifest. In this way, the image presented in this discourse can serve as an inspiration and encouragement when having to face strong *vedanā*s. However strong the wind of *vedanā* may blow, sooner or later it will abate.

THE GUESTHOUSE

The next discourse presents another metaphor that can be employed in ways similar to the previous one describing different winds in the sky. The present illustration concerns a guesthouse:[27]

> It is just as various types of people who stay in a guesthouse: warriors, brahmins, householders, people from the countryside, hunters, those who keep the precepts, those who break the precepts, those who live at home, and those who are homeless; all come to stay therein.
>
> This body is also just like that [guesthouse]. Various types of *vedanās* arise one after the other: unpleasant *vedanās*, pleasant *vedanās*, or neutral *vedanās*;
>
> pleasant bodily *vedanās*, unpleasant bodily *vedanās*, and neutral bodily *vedanās*; pleasant mental *vedanās*, unpleasant mental *vedanās*, and neutral mental *vedanās*;
>
> worldly pleasant *vedanās*, worldly unpleasant *vedanās*, worldly neutral *vedanās*; unworldly pleasant *vedanās*, unworldly unpleasant *vedanās*, and unworldly neutral *vedanās*;
>
> pleasant *vedanās* [related to] passionate attachment, unpleasant *vedanās* [related to] passionate attachment, and neutral *vedanās* [related to] passionate attachment; pleasant *vedanās* [related to] renunciation, unpleasant *vedanās* [related to] renunciation, and neutral *vedanās* [related to] renunciation.

The Pāli parallel (SN 36.14) mentions warriors, brahmins, merchants, and workers who come from any of the four directions to stay in the guesthouse. These are the four main classes or castes of Indian society and thereby stand representative of the variety of guests that could come to a guesthouse. The *Saṃyutta-nikāya* version does not have a counterpart to the additional distinctions made in the discourse translated above, namely between those who either keep or else break the precepts, as well as between lay people and those who have gone forth, and it also does not mention people from the countryside and hunters.

In relation to the different *vedanās* that these guests serve to illustrate, only the distinction into the three affective types of *vedanā* and their further analysis into worldly and unworldly occurrences are shared by the two versions. These two types of analysis are also part of the scheme of contemplation of *vedanās* that is common to the *Satipaṭṭhāna-sutta* and its two Chinese *Āgama* parallels: the three affective tones combined with the distinction between worldly and unworldly.[28] I will return to this distinction in a subsequent part of my exploration (see below p. 36).

From a practical viewpoint, the present discourse can be taken as an invitation to play the role of a friendly but uninvolved host, knowing only too well that whoever comes to stay will again depart. This makes it meaningless to get excited because of the nature of a particular guest. Some may be rather nice, others quite unpleasant. They all come and go. Similarly, some *vedanās* can be rather pleasant, others quite painful. No need to get excited about them. They will all go of their own accord. In this way, here as well as elsewhere, awareness of the impermanent nature of *vedanā* provides a tool for fostering the growth of liberating insight.

THE IMPORT OF *DUKKHA*

A key aspect of liberating insight in early Buddhist thought is the understanding that what is impermanent necessarily must be *dukkha*, in the sense of being unable to provide lasting satisfaction. The implications of the term *dukkha* in this context differ from what the same Pāli term conveys when used to designate one of the three types of *vedanā*, namely those that are "painful." The need to differentiate such usages of the term *dukkha* comes up in a question posed by the Buddha's attendant Ānanda to his teacher in the following manner:[29]

> [Ānanda] said to the Buddha: "Blessed One, being alone in a quiet place meditating and reflecting, I had this thought: 'The Blessed One has taught three *vedanās* one after the other, as pleasant *vedanās*, unpleasant *vedanās*, or neutral *vedanās*; and he has also taught that all *vedanās* are entirely *dukkha*. What is the meaning of this?'"
>
> The Buddha said to Ānanda: "It is on account of the impermanence of all formations, on account of the changing nature of all formations, that I stated that whatever is felt is completely *dukkha*. Furthermore, Ānanda, I have stated it on account of the gradual appeasement of all formations, and I have stated it on account of the gradual tranquilization of all formations that all *vedanās* are completely *dukkha*."
>
> Ānanda said to the Buddha: "Blessed One, in what way have you stated it on account of the gradual appeasement of all formations?"[30]
>
> The Buddha said to Ānanda: "At the time of attaining the first absorption, [the formations of] speech are

appeased; at the time of attaining the second absorption,
[directed] awareness and [sustained] contemplation are
appeased; at the time of attaining the third absorption,
mental joy is appeased; at the time of attaining the
fourth absorption, breathing in and out is appeased;
at the time of attaining the sphere of [boundless]
space, perceptions of form are appeased; at the time
of attaining the sphere of [boundless] consciousness,
the perception of the sphere of [boundless] space
is appeased; at the time of attaining the sphere of
nothingness, the perception of the sphere of [boundless]
consciousness is appeased; at the time of attaining the
sphere of neither perception nor non-perception, the
perception of the sphere of nothingness is appeased; at
the time of attaining the cessation of perceptions and
vedanā, perceptions and *vedanās* are appeased. This is
called the gradual appeasement of formations.

The questioner in the Pāli version (SN 36.11) is an
unnamed monk. The *Saṃyutta-nikāya* discourse also
differs by presenting the eradication of all defilements
as the culmination point. The Chinese parallel makes a
similar point at the end of its presentation, after having
expounded the tranquilization of formations in the
same manner as the appeasement of formations.

The gradual progression described in both versions
proceeds through the four absorptions and the four
immaterial attainments up to the attainment of cessation,
where all experiencing of *vedanās* ceases. Although all of
the preceding experiences, however refined, fall within the
scope of *dukkha*, at the same time none of them involves the
experience of unpleasant *vedanās*. In this way, the gradual
refinement serves as an illustration of the dictum that all
vedanās fall within the scope of *dukkha*. At the same time,

the teaching delineates a meditative progression that will eventually lead beyond all *dukkha*.

The dictum as such is of considerable importance for appreciating the meaning of the term *dukkha* as a qualification of conditioned phenomena in general. Although regularly translated as "suffering," this rendering fails to do justice to the different dimensions of this Pāli term in its early Buddhist usage.

Just to recapitulate, one of these dimensions is indeed the experience of pain, where *dukkha* stands for one of the three *vedanā*s, namely those that are unpleasant. Yet, the experience of pain does not invariably result in suffering. The simile of the two darts, discussed above, illustrates this well. The first dart of physical pain need not be followed by the additional dart of mental suffering. By training in mindfulness, it becomes possible to face the challenge of pain with a balanced mind. This is based on learning to avoid reactions of craving for the pain to disappear and then of suffering when this does not happen in accordance with one's wishes. Hence *dukkha* as one of the three *vedanā*s refers to what is "unpleasant," at times even what is "painful," but this does not invariably result in "suffering."

Another dimension of the same Pāli term concerns all conditioned phenomena, and it is this usage which the above discourse clarifies. All conditioned phenomena can without exception be qualified as *dukkha*. This usage thereby covers all three types of *vedanā*, as conditioned phenomena can be experienced as pleasant, unpleasant, or neither of the two.

Now pleasant experiences could hardly be considered "suffering." Of course, what is pleasant will eventually change, but so do painful experiences and in that case a change can be perceived as positive. Therefore, the fact of change cannot unequivocally be considered as productive of suffering.

Pleasant experiences are pleasant, but they fail to give lasting satisfaction. Hence *dukkha*, when applied to all conditioned phenomena, and therewith to any *vedanā*, could better be rendered as "unsatisfactory." Whatever *vedanā* is experienced, it cannot yield lasting satisfaction, simply by dint of its impermanent nature. For this reason, anything that is conditioned (and therefore changing) is indeed unsatisfactory.

In contrast, "suffering" is not a quality shared by all conditioned phenomena. Instead, it is the reaction of an untrained mind. For this reason, the term "suffering" is not a qualification applicable to all conditioned phenomena. The computer right in front of me, as I write these lines, is not suffering. It lacks sentience and cannot suffer, and whether I suffer because of it depends on my attachment to it. But the computer is definitely *dukkha*, because it cannot give me truly lasting satisfaction.

Keeping this basic clarification in mind can be of considerable importance for actual practice. The pervasive applicability of *dukkha* does not mean that everything should now be viewed in a negative light and the more depressed we become the deeper must be our understanding of the Buddha's teachings. Instead, genuine insight into *dukkha* leads to a shift in perspective toward finding true happiness within, by cultivating the qualities that lead to the happiness of an increasingly more liberated mind.

INSIGHT IN A NUTSHELL

The next passage presents a series of key questions regarding insight into the nature of *vedanā*. These key questions, which the discourse presents as part of a pre-awakening reflection of the Buddha, take the following form:[31]

What are [the types of] *vedanā*? What is the arising of *vedanā*? What is the cessation of *vedanā*? What is the path to the arising of *vedanā*? What is the path to the cessation of *vedanā*? What is the gratification in *vedanā*? What is the disadvantage in *vedanā*? What is the release from *vedanā*? He examined in this way:

There are three *vedanās*: pleasant *vedanā*, unpleasant *vedanā*, and neutral *vedanā*. The arising of contact is the arising of *vedanā*; the cessation of contact is the cessation of *vedanā*.

Craving with delight for *vedanā*, extolling it, being defiled by attachment to it, taking a firm stance on it, this is called the path to the arising of *vedanā*. Not craving with delight for *vedanā*, extolling it, being defiled by attachment to it, taking a firm stance on it, this is called the path to the cessation of *vedanā*.

The joy and delight that arises in dependence on *vedanā*, this is called the gratification in *vedanā*. The nature of *vedanā* to be impermanent and to change, this is called the disadvantage in *vedanā*. The abandoning of desire and passion for *vedanā*, the going beyond desire and passion, this is called the release from *vedanā*.

The Pāli parallel (SN 36.24) equates the path to the cessation of *vedanā* with the eightfold path. This provides a broader context for the basic task of stepping out of craving and attachment. Whichever of these two complementary definitions of the path is adopted, the above survey presents liberating insight into *vedanā* in a nutshell.

Based on the fundamental distinction of the three affective tones, insight into the conditionality of *vedanā* as something that arises based on contact builds the foundation for the task of stepping out of craving. This task can benefit from adopting the three perspectives of gratification (literally "taste"), disadvantage (literally "danger"), and release (literally "escape"). There is indeed gratification to be found in *vedanā*, but this comes inexorably intertwined with the disadvantage that, sooner or later, the gratification is going to end due to the law of impermanence. The extent to which we developed attachment during the gratification stage determines to what extent we will suffer when what was pleasant changes to neutral or even unpleasant. For this reason, the task of stepping out of craving (or desire and passion) is the way out; it provides an escape or release from the predicament of being enslaved by *vedanā*.

The next discourses offer the same exposition on the nature of *vedanā*, with the only difference being that, instead of reporting a pre-awakening reflection of the Buddha, the questions are part of a dialogue between the Buddha and his monastic disciples.[32] From a practical viewpoint, these different modalities of the same basic instruction can be taken as an encouragement to consider the above teaching relevant to meditators in general, rather than being something pertinent only to the Buddha's pre-awakening practice. On this understanding, the series of questions can be employed as a way of providing a framework for insightful reflection that can inform actual meditation practice. Based on mindfully discerning the three types of *vedanā*, the main lines of inquiry would be:

What is the immediate cause for the arising of this particular *vedanā*?

What keeps fueling the arising of this *vedanā*?

How to find release in relation to this *vedanā*?

The first query leads to the identification of a particular contact as the key condition for *vedanā* to arise. The second question drives home the fact that craving keeps fueling such arising. In this way, from the viewpoint of the standard exposition of dependent arising, the preceding condition of contact and the ensuing condition of craving have been covered. Based on having situated *vedanā* in its causal nexus in this way, the possibility opens up of finding release from *vedanā*. This requires contextualizing any gratification experienced through *vedanā* by turning awareness to the unavoidable disadvantage inherent in the changing nature of *vedanā*. Such insight can safely be expected to have a remarkable liberating potential.

True Renunciants

The next discourse clarifies that the crucial understanding of the nature of *vedanā*, described in the discourse taken up above, is actually required even for recluses and brahmins in general, if they wish to deserve the appellation by which they were known in the ancient Indian setting:[33]

> If recluses and brahmins know all *vedanā*s as they really are, know as it really is the arising of *vedanā*s, the cessation of *vedanā*s, the path to the arising of *vedanā*s, the path to the cessation of *vedanā*s, the gratification in *vedanā*s, the disadvantage in *vedanā*s, and the release from *vedanā*s, then these are recluses among recluses, these are brahmins among brahmins, they conform to being recluses, they conform to being brahmins, they are of the substance of recluses, they are of the substance of brahmins. They will realize here and now, knowing for themselves: "Birth for me has been eradicated, the holy life has been established, what had to be done has been done, I myself know that there will be no receiving of any further existence."

The final part about realizing that birth has been eradicated, etc., is a standard description of the final goal in the early discourses. In addition to showing in this way how penetrative insight into *vedanā*s leads all the way to full awakening, the above passage and its Pāli parallel (SN 36.26) also describe recluses and brahmins who do not have such knowledge and for this reason do not deserve to be truly reckoned recluses and brahmins. This can be understood to convey that penetrative insight into *vedanā* can truly engender inner renunciation. In other words, such insight can be expected to reduce and eventually remove passion and attachments, as a way to becoming indeed a true renunciant.

In this way, the present passage highlights again the general relevance and applicability of the basic teaching on the nature of *vedanā*. This takes the form of combining a perspective modeled on the scheme of the four noble truths (*dukkha*, its arising, its cessation, and the path to its cessation) with the threefold perspective based on discerning gratification, disadvantage, and release.[34]

WORLDLY AND UNWORLDLY

The distinction of *vedanā* into worldly and unworldly types forms an important dimension of the instruction for contemplation of *vedanās* in the *Satipaṭṭhāna-sutta* and its two Chinese *Āgama* parallels. The implications of this distinction can be appreciated with the help of the following explanation:[35]

> What is worldly joy? That is, joy arisen and delight arisen in dependence on the five [types of] sensual pleasures: this is called worldly joy.
>
> What is unworldly joy? That is, delight and joy arisen from concentration by calming [directed] awareness and [sustained] contemplation, being with inner confidence and unification of the mind, being without [directed] awareness and without [sustained] contemplation: this is called unworldly joy.
>
> What is more unworldly than unworldly joy? That is, [when] a monastic dwells free from delight and passion, with an equanimous mind, with right mindfulness, and with right knowledge, dwelling at peace in what those noble ones declare to be equanimity: this is called more unworldly than unworldly joy.

The Pāli version (SN 36.29) treats the case of unworldly joy by referring to the experience of the first and the second absorption. The presence of non-sensual joy is indeed a shared quality of these two concentrative experiences. The Chinese parallel translated above only mentions the standard description of the second absorption. Here the Pāli version offers a more convincing presentation, in that the joy that arises from concentration up to and including the level of the second absorption can be reckoned to be of an unworldly type.

A significant difference emerges in relation to more unworldly than unworldly joy. The description in the *Saṃyukta-āgama* discourse seems to intend the mental quality achieved with the third absorption. The *Saṃyutta-nikāya* parallel instead depicts the joy experienced when full awakening has been attained and the mind is completely freed from all defilements. Here, again, the Pāli presentation appears to be more to the point than the passage translated above. That the supreme type of joy comes from full awakening is in fact confirmed in the next discourse in the *Saṃyukta-āgama*. The two versions report a monastic stating that the supreme joy or happiness is to be found in the experience of absorption (according to the Chinese) or in the celestial realm corresponding to the third absorption (according to the Pāli version). Ānanda corrects this proposal, considering as supreme the joy or happiness related to gaining the destruction of the influxes.[36] The position taken in these two parallel versions supports the impression that more unworldly than unworldly joy should be related to awakening rather than to absorption attainment.

In both versions, sensual pleasures derived from experiences through the five senses clearly illustrate the case of worldly joy. At first sight, this might give the impression that the difference between worldly and unworldly can be mapped onto the distinction between sensory and mental. Yet, closer inspection shows that this is not the case. In fact, the qualification "unworldly" could hardly intend "mental" in contrast to "sensory," as the phrase "more unworldly than unworldly" would then qualify experiences as "more mental than mental." Such an idea fails to make sense.

A proper appreciation of the implications of the qualification "worldly" can benefit from clearly distinguishing
what is "sensual" from what is "sensory." Fully awakened
ones still experience the whole range of sensory experiences. Yet, they do so without sensual desire. The problem
of sensuality is not a property of the objects of the senses
themselves. Instead, it describes an unskillful mental
reaction toward them.

Joy of an unworldly type in turn finds illustration in
the experience of deep concentration up to the level of
the second absorption. This suggests that the distinction
between what is worldly and what is unworldly relates to
the quality of the mind in which joy occurs, in particular in
terms of the possible activation of an underlying tendency.

Of further interest here are the *Kāyagatāsati-sutta*
and its parallel, which include the experience of the
absorptions in a range of practices related to mindfulness
of the body. According to the relevant passages, with the
first and second absorptions a practitioner's whole body
is thoroughly pervaded with joy and happiness.[37] These
texts clearly consider these absorptions to be embodied
experiences, which confirms that qualifying an absorption
as "unworldly" does not refer to being apart from all of the
physical senses. This holds even though the experience of
the body in deep concentration can safely be considered
to differ substantially from the way the body is sensed in
daily life.

In sum, sensuality arouses worldly pleasant *vedanā*s,
whereas the lower absorptions arouse unworldly pleasant
*vedanā*s. In this way, the distinction of *vedanā*s into worldly
and unworldly types can serve as a tool to direct attention to
the overall quality of the mind, in the sense of investigating
whether it is related to sensuality or its absence. In other

words, in the case of joyful *vedanā* this distinction relates to the question of the underlying tendency to passion.

The discourse translated above and its Pāli parallel apply the same basic distinction between what is worldly and what is unworldly also to experiences characterized by neutral *vedanās* (here referred to as types of equanimity). Although not explicitly mentioned, the same could also be related to unpleasant *vedanās*. In each case, the difference revolves around the respective underlying tendency and hence around the ethical quality of the mind within which a particular *vedanā* arises.

In the case of the *Satipaṭṭhāna-sutta* and its parallels, then, based on directing mindfulness to the affective quality of the three types of *vedanā*, the additional distinction of these into worldly and unworldly types prepares the ground for the next *satipaṭṭhāna* of contemplation of the mind. It already alerts the meditator to the need to pay attention to the overall quality of the mind, in particular to the crucial question: Is the mind now in a wholesome or unwholesome condition?

MANY TYPES

Besides differentiating between worldly and unworldly types, several other distinctions can be made in relation to *vedanā*. A survey of such alternatives comes up in another discourse, which begins by reporting a dispute between two disciples of the Buddha. One of the two insisted that the Buddha had taught three types of *vedanā*, whereas the other firmly advocated that the Buddha had much rather taught two types of *vedanā*.[38] In response to being informed of this dispute, the Buddha clarified that he had taught various ways of analyzing *vedanā*, making it meaningless to insist on one of these ways as the only right one. The Pāli versions of this discourse (MN 59 and SN 36.19) just provide a list of the different types of *vedanā*, without spelling out their implications.[39] This list mentions two, three, five, six, eighteen, thirty-six, and one hundred and eight *vedanās*.

The Chinese and Tibetan parallels, however, not only have additional items in their lists (one, four, and innumerable types of *vedanā*), they also follow this list by explaining what each category refers to. A similar explanation (for the types of *vedanā* common to all versions) can also be found in another Pāli discourse.[40] This means that, though absent from the Pāli parallels to the *Saṃyukta-āgama* passage translated below, the basic ideas are attested in the Pāli tradition as well. The listing of types of *vedanā* and the respective explanations in the *Saṃyukta-āgama* version proceed as follows:[41]

> At times I have taught one *vedanā*, at other times I have taught two *vedanās*, or I have taught three, four, five, six, eighteen, thirty-six, and up to one hundred

and eight *vedanās*, and at other times I have taught innumerable *vedanās*.

What is the one *vedanā* I have taught? As I have taught, whatever is felt is all *dukkha*. This is called the one *vedanā* I have taught.

What are the two *vedanās* I have taught? I have taught bodily *vedanās* and mental *vedanās*. These are called the two *vedanās* [I have taught].

What are the three *vedanās* [I have taught]? They are pleasant *vedanās*, unpleasant *vedanās*, and neutral *vedanās*. [These are called the three *vedanās* I have taught.]

What are the four *vedanās* [I have taught]? That is, they are *vedanās* in bondage to the element of sensuality, *vedanās* in bondage to the element of form, *vedanās* in bondage to the element of the formless,[42] and *vedanās* that are without bondage.[43] [These are called the four *vedanās* I have taught.]

What are the five *vedanās* I have taught? That is, they are the faculty of [bodily] pleasure, the faculty of [mental] delight, the faculty of [bodily] pain, the faculty of [mental] sadness, and the faculty of equanimity. These are called the five *vedanās* I have taught.

What are the six *vedanās* I have taught? That is, they are *vedanās* arisen from eye-contact and *vedanās* arisen from ear-, nose-, tongue-, body-, and mind-contact. [These are called the six *vedanās* I have taught.]

What are the eighteen *vedanās* I have taught? That is, they are six ways of pursuing joy, six ways of pursuing sadness, and six ways of pursuing equanimity. These are called the eighteen *vedanās* I have taught.

What are the thirty-six *vedanās* [I have taught]? They are joy in dependence on the six [modes of] passionate attachment, joy in dependence on the six [modes of] being free from passionate attachment, sadness in dependence on the six [modes of] passionate attachment, sadness in dependence on the six [modes of] being free from passionate attachment, equanimity in dependence on the six [modes of] passionate attachment, and equanimity in dependence on the six [modes of] being free from passionate attachment. These are called the thirty-six *vedanā*s I have taught.

What are the one hundred and eight *vedanā*s I have taught? That is, they are the thirty-six [types of] *vedanā* [in the three periods of time:] the thirty-six [types of] the past, the thirty-six [types of] the future, and the thirty-six [types of] the present. These are called the one hundred and eight *vedanā*s I have taught.

What are the innumerable *vedanā*s I have taught? As I have taught, there is this *vedanā* and that *vedanā*, etc. In this way, these are said to be innumerable. These are called the innumerable *vedanā*s I have taught.

Regarding what the version translated above introduces as "one" type of *vedanā*, it could be objected that the qualification of all *vedanā*s as *dukkha* is precisely not about a type of *vedanā*, but much rather concerns the unsatisfactory quality of all that is felt. Again, speaking of innumerable types of *vedanā* does not really serve any specific purpose, as it does not yield a tool capable of discerning different types of *vedanā*s. Overall, the presentation in the above passage seems to reflect a shift from practice-related interests to more descriptive concerns, a feature that becomes increasingly prominent with the growth of Abhidhamma exegesis.[44] The Pāli version is in comparison more to the point.

Unlike the one and the innumerable types, mentioned in the above passage, the categories shared by the parallel versions do have a practical relevance. The significance of discerning *vedanās* into "two" types, bodily and mental, can be appreciated by recourse to the simile of the dart, mentioned above (p. 19). The realization that the bodily *vedanās* of pain do not have to lead to the additional dart of mental suffering and its host of unpleasant *vedanās* can have a remarkably transformative effect. The nature of human bodies is such that sooner or later they will give rise to pain. Hence the importance of finding a way of facing such pain can hardly be overestimated.

The "three" affective tones of *vedanā* are the most often mentioned way of analysis in the discourses. The popularity of this analysis probably reflects its potential in helping to recognize the potential triggering of one of the three corresponding underlying tendencies. For this reason, it is a central task of mindfulness to be aware of these three tones in order to enable a watchful presence at the very outset of unwholesome reactions.

The "four" types, which are not taken up in the Pāli parallel, reflect the increasing subtlety of bondage to *vedanās*, which can be to sensuality, to form, and to formlessness, together with those related to freedom from bondage.

The "five" faculties can be understood to combine the two and three types already mentioned in a particular way, namely by dividing pleasant and unpleasant experiences into mental and bodily types. Neutral experiences are not divided in a like manner, perhaps because a division into bodily and mental types is particularly relevant when experiencing pleasure or pain. If this interpretation is granted, it would imply that it is sufficient for mindful contemplation of neutral *vedanās* to ensure recognition, which in itself is already a step against the current of ignorance. The division into bodily and mental types, reflecting the understanding of whether a particular *vedanā* was caused by physical circumstances or mental reactivity, is in turn particularly fruitful for facing the extremes in the range of felt experience, the peaks of bliss and the nadirs of pain.

The conditionality of *vedanās* appears to be central to the listing of "six" types, drawing attention to which of the six sense doors was responsible for the particular *vedanā* that arose. Sustained contemplation undertaken along the lines of this particular distinction can reveal personal preferences or tendencies. Some are more easily enchanted by what is seen, others get particularly carried away by what is heard, and others may find a comparable emphasis in relation to smells, tastes, tangibles, or purely mental occurrences. Knowing our own propensities can help to beware of the potential impact of *vedanās* in leading to unskillful reactions.

A combination of this sixfold distinction with the analysis into three affective tones then yields the "eighteen" types of *vedanā*. This can be read as an invitation to deepen the appreciation gained through the sixfold distinction by watching how this plays out for pleasant, unpleasant, and neutral experience at each sense door.

Building on the combination of the sixfold distinction according to the senses with the three affective types then comes the division of each of these according to their ethical quality in terms of being with or without attachment, yielding an overall count of "thirty-six." This points to what, in the end, is perhaps the most crucial question: Is the *vedanā* experienced right now with attachment or does it occur in the absence of attachment?

This same crucial question can be posed not only in relation to what happens right now, but also retrospectively in relation to the past, and even prospectively in relation to what can reasonably be expected to happen in the future. With this broadening of perspective along the temporal axis, the auspicious count of one hundred and eight is reached. Although this may seem a rather complex tool at first sight, it can be helpful to keep in mind that the crucial question remains whether attachment is present or absent. The rest of the analysis into one hundred and eight types can then be understood to make it clear that this basic inquiry is relevant at all times and in relation to any experience.

Based on the above survey of types of *vedanā* and on pointing out that it is meaningless to take a dogmatic stance on any of these as the only right one, the parallel versions continue by depicting a series of increasingly sublime types of happiness. Proceeding beyond the lowly happiness of sensuality, these are the ever more subtle and superior forms of happiness that can be experienced by progressively attaining the four absorptions and the four immaterial spheres. The parallels agree in taking this beyond the highest immaterial sphere of neither-perception-nor-non-perception to the attainment of the cessation of perceptions and *vedanās*:[45]

> By completely going beyond the sphere of neither-perception-nor-non-perception, one dwells endowed with the direct realization of the cessation of perceptions and *vedanās*. This is called a superior happiness that goes beyond that.

In short, the early Buddhist conception of happiness is such that its peak goes beyond the experience of *vedanā*.

KARMA

Although the previous discourse has surveyed a broad range of different types of *vedanā*, even this much is not an exhaustive account of all of its possible variations. This can be seen in the discourse taken up presently, which is no longer part of the collected discourses on the topic of *vedanā* in the Chinese *Saṃyukta-āgama*.[46] The Pāli parallel (SN 36.21), however, does occur in the section on *vedanā*s in the *Saṃyutta-nikāya*. The key question taken up in the different versions of this discourse is a proposal made by some recluses and brahmins that all *vedanā*s arise due to karma. The Buddha expressed his clear disagreement with such a position:[47]

> When those recluses and brahmins proclaim that everything that is known and felt by a person has its origin entirely in formerly created conditions, they have relinquished what is a matter of truth in the world and follow their own views; they make false statements.

The untenability of such a proposal finds an illustration in the example of *vedanā*s originating from various bodily disorders or else from the body being afflicted, be this out of carelessness (as in the Pāli version), by the undertaking of ascetic practices (as in the *Saṃyukta-āgama* parallels), or else from being harmed by others. All these count as potential causes for the experience of *vedanā*, in addition to past karma.

Of course, due to not having reached liberation in the past one still has a body now. From this perspective, one could argue that anything that happens to the body is the result of the past karma of not having gone beyond rebirth in a human body. The point made in the present passage is different, however, as its target is karmic determinism. This goes beyond acknowledging that the past influences the present and proposes that whatever happens at present is without exception due to something done in the past. This is not the case. Although the past definitely has its impact, it is not the sole determinant of what happens now.

The position taken in this way sets early Buddhist thought apart from some ascetic practitioners in ancient India, in particular those of the Jain tradition, who believed that the path to liberation required expiating one's former bad deeds by inflicting pain on oneself. The early Buddhist perspective differs. Although some pain will indeed be the result of former karma, the key to liberation lies not in enduring it as a form of expiation but much rather in turning its experience into an occasion for arousing insight.

THE PAIN OF DISEASE

How to face the pain of disease with mindfulness and insight is the theme of the next passage to be taken up, whose Pāli parallel (SN 36.7) still forms part of the collected discourses on *vedanā*. The setting is a visit by the Buddha to the monastic sick ward, occasioning the following instruction:[48]

> To one who is in this way with right mindfulness and right knowledge, unpleasant *vedanās* arise dependent on conditions, not independent of conditions. What are the conditions on which they depend? They depend in this way on the body. One reflects: "This body of mine is impermanent, produced by [former] volitions,[49] arisen in dependence on conditions. Unpleasant *vedanās* are also impermanent, produced by [former] volitions, arisen in dependence on conditions."
>
> One contemplates the body and unpleasant *vedanās* as impermanent ... up to ... [contemplates] relinquishing. The underlying tendency to aversion in relation to these unpleasant *vedanās* will no longer affect one.[50]

The same basic pattern applies to pleasant and neutral *vedanās*, with the difference that such contemplation leads respectively beyond the underlying tendencies to sensual desire and ignorance.

From a practical perspective, the key remains awareness of impermanence, together with conditionality. It is remarkable how, time and again, the discourses that provide insight perspectives on *vedanā* build around this central theme of impermanence. In both versions, contemplation of impermanence then leads via dispassion and cessation (abbreviated in the Chinese original translated above) to relinquishing or letting go.

This progression is central for liberating insight and is found similarly in the final part of the instructions on mindfulness of breathing.[51] Briefly stated, insight into impermanence leads on to dispassion, in the sense of letting the implications of the fact that everything keeps changing all the time really sink into the mind and transform its affective disposition through a gradual reduction of passionate attachments. Why become passionate for things that anyway will not last? Growing dispassion diminishes the ingrained tendency to want only what is new and beginning, at the cost of ignoring what is old and ending, and there can be an inner sense of ease with the cessation of phenomena. This is in a way the cutting edge of impermanence, namely that it invariably leads to vanishing and disappearing. Contemplating cessation in this way fosters increasing willingness to let go, by way of relinquishing all clinging and grasping at what will pass away anyway. This is how the underlying tendencies can gradually be deactivated until eventually, with a most complete letting go of all and everything, they can be eradicated.

MINDFUL EATING

By way of complementing the different perspectives on liberating insight that have emerged so far, another passage can be taken up that relates *vedanā* to a daily-life activity and purpose: mindful eating to know one's measure with food and thereby achieve a reduction of overweight. Perhaps somewhat unexpectedly, such instructions can already be found among the early discourses. The relevant passage begins with an overweight king visiting the Buddha. On seeing the king's condition, the Buddha offers the following advice:[52]

> People should collect themselves with mindfulness,
> Knowing their measure with each meal.
> This then decreases their *vedanās*;
> They digest easily and guard their longevity.

The parallel versions agree in reporting that this instruction had its effect, as the king indeed learnt to know his measure, reduce his excessive food intake, and thereby achieve a reduction in weight. This goes to show that the employment of mindfulness for health purposes is not merely a recent invention but was already in use in ancient India.[53]

From a practical perspective, the above instruction can be taken as an invitation to extend contemplation of *vedanās* to mealtimes. The task would simply be to remain aware of the sensations experienced when eating, in particular noting when one's measure has been reached rather than being carried away by the taste or by distractions and continuing to eat beyond what is actually required.

A source of inspiration for such practice could be the Buddha himself. The *Brahmāyu-sutta* and its parallel report that the Buddha experienced the taste of the food without experiencing passion for the taste.[54] This goes to show that tasting as such is not a problem; in fact, it is part of the digestive process. The problem is when such tasting leads to, or occurs in conjunction with, attachment and passion; in other words, when the *vedanā*s of taste trigger an underlying tendency.

Viewed from this perspective, then, eating can become an occasion for continuing the meditative work against the power of the underlying tendencies. The potential of bringing mindfulness to bear on the topic of partaking of food emerges from the following indication:[55]

> Having penetrative understanding of material food, passionate craving for the five strands of sensual pleasures is then abandoned. Passionate craving for the five strands of sensual pleasures being abandoned, I do not see in that learned noble disciple a single underlying fetter in relation to the five strands of sensual pleasures which has not been abandoned, a single fetter such that, due to being bound by it, there is a returning to being born in this world.

The Pāli version (SN 12.63) makes basically the same point. The reference to not coming back to this world points to the attainment of at least the third level of awakening, non-return. This goes to show that mindful eating, besides its potential to reduce weight, can also make a rather substantial contribution to reducing the weight of defilements in the mind.

This completes my survey of relevant passages from the *Saṃyukta-āgama*, and in what follows I turn to material found in the other three Chinese *Āgama*s, beginning with the collection of long discourses, the *Dīrgha-āgama*.

Dependent Arising

The first of the discourses to be taken up from the *Dīrgha-āgama* presents a detailed examination of the principle of "dependent arising" (*paṭicca samuppāda*), which repeatedly came up in one way or another in the passages surveyed above. The present occasion thereby affords me an opportunity to explore in more details this principle, which stands at the heart of the Dhamma, the Buddha's teaching. According to a well-known saying, one who sees dependent arising sees the Dhamma, and conversely one who sees the Dhamma sees dependent arising.[56] What such seeing requires, however, is perhaps not necessarily obvious. In order to unpack this statement and relate it to the meditative contemplation of *vedanās*, first of all it could be noted that a chief principle behind expositions of dependent arising is the principle of specific conditionality.[57] Simply said, this means that there are specific conditions required for something to arise. In the absence of the relevant specific condition(s), that which depends on them will cease or not even arise in the first place.

A straightforward illustration can be taken from the final part of a standard exposition of dependent arising by way of twelve links. The final part states that birth is the condition for old age and death (together with other manifestations of *dukkha*). Birth is a specific condition for old age and death because, without birth, old age and death will not manifest. The same basic principle of specific conditionality then applies to each of the standard twelve links, which are as follows:

ignorance
volitional formations
consciousness
name-and-form
six sense spheres
contact
vedanā
craving
clinging
becoming
birth
aging-and-death

The formulation of this particular series of links is best understood to stand in response to a Vedic creation myth.[58] This means that the twelve links can be considered as one particularly prominent expression of dependent arising, presumably occurring so frequently because it resonated with ideas prevalent in the ancient Indian setting. In other words, this specific formulation would have served to create a sense of familiarity, while at the same time completely reversing the original meaning of its apparent Vedic antecedent. Instead of leading to the creation of the world, the Buddhist teaching on dependent arising reveals the creation of *dukkha*. Moreover, in the cessation mode, where the cessation of each link leads to the cessation of the next, the same teaching shows how to get out of all 'creation.'

Keeping in mind the central importance of the basic principle of specific conditionality provides a helpful perspective on the existence of various alternative formulations, found in the discourses, which involve fewer than the standard twelve links. These are expressions of the same basic principle and are just as valid as the twelve-link formula. What matters from a practical perspective, in the end, is to identify the specific conditions that lead to *dukkha* and to bring about their cessation.

This assessment in turn puts the spotlight on the role of *vedanā* as the necessary condition for craving. Out of the whole series of links listed above, the repercussions of this particular specific condition can hardly be overestimated, wherefore it presents a crucial opportunity for the cultivation of liberating insight.

Fully awakened ones, arahants, still experience contact leading to *vedanā*. The same no longer holds for what happens from this point onward, as fully awakened ones will not react to *vedanā* with craving. Clearly, the specific conditionality at this juncture carries considerable importance.

The task is to be mindful of *vedanā* in order to bring into the full view of attention what happens at this juncture. This helps avoid that the tendrils of ignorance, the initial specific condition in the series of the dependent arising of *dukkha*, activate craving in relation to whatever *vedanā* is experienced. All that is required is to become fully aware of the push of *vedanā* toward reaction, mindfully noting it without acting it out. In this way, the cultivation of mindfulness can introduce a crucial pause, which enables a full appreciation of the situation rather than responding on the spot to the affective push of *vedanā* by way of craving for more of this and less of that. From the viewpoint of the path to liberation, it is difficult to think of something that could be of greater importance than mindfully avoiding the arising of craving in order to side-step and eventually completely overcome *dukkha*.

Yet, this much does not yet exhaust the role of *vedanā* in the context of the dependent arising. Another role emerges in relation to the link of name-and-form, as "name" comprises *vedanā*. Here, name stands for those mental factors that are involved in naming things, in the construction of concepts and labels required to recognize and mentally process the raw data of experience. Besides *vedanā*, these mental factors are perception (*saññā*), volition (*cetanā*), contact (*phassa*), and attention (*manasikāra*);[59] be it noted that here consciousness is not part of name.

This additional occurrence of *vedanā* as part of name in the context of dependent arising provides a helpful background for considering a passage in the *Mahānidāna-sutta*, the Great Discourse on Conditionality (DN 15). In addition to the Pāli version of what among the early discourses is the longest and most detailed exposition on the topic of dependent arising or conditionality, several parallels are extant in Chinese translation. One of these, found in a *Dīrgha-āgama* collection (the term *Dīrgha-āgama* being a near equivalent to the Pāli *Dīgha-nikāya*, both standing for a collection of long discourses), proceeds as follows:[60]

> Ānanda, therefore, name-and-form conditions consciousness, consciousness conditions name-and-form, name-and-form conditions the six sense spheres, the six sense spheres condition contact, contact conditions *vedanā*, *vedanā* conditions craving, craving conditions clinging, clinging conditions becoming, becoming conditions birth, birth conditions old age, death, sadness, sorrow, pain, and vexations: the arising of the great mass of *dukkha*.

Particularly significant in this presentation is the reciprocal conditioning relationship between consciousness and name-and-form.[61] Another discourse illustrates this relationship with the example of two bundles of reeds that stand leaning on each other.[62] Each needs the other in order to be able to stand up.

The reciprocal conditioning between consciousness and name-and-form can be taken to explain the continuity of existence, during life as well as from one life to another.[63] One of the two bundles of reeds represents the process of being conscious. The other bundle of reeds stands for the mental factors and activities that make sense of things, giving them a 'name,' which occur in conjunction with 'form' as the experience of materiality. In this context, *vedanā* is part of name as what makes sense of things, here in particular in its role of providing an affective tone to experience as being pleasant, or unpleasant, or else neutral.

From the viewpoint of actual meditation practice, what emerges in this way could be explored by broadening the attentional field while observing *vedanās*. Such broadening of perspective could take the form of letting the process of being conscious of *vedanā* stand out more clearly in the field of meditative awareness. In the case of bodily pain, for example, the pain itself is an object of the sense door of the body. Meditative attention can simply be directed to knowing that tactile experience. But it is also possible to include the corresponding body-consciousness in the range of meditative observation by broadening the scope of awareness to include the knowing of the bodily pain. Doing so enables a more in-depth appreciation of the dependently arisen nature of experience at the bodily sense door. A side-effect of such practice that has considerable practical importance is that the mind's tendency to get lost in distraction is more easily and swiftly noted.

The same principle of including the respective type of consciousness in the purview of one's meditative vision can be applied to any sense door and its corresponding type of *vedanā*. In addition to noting the *vedanā* itself, it is possible to be also aware of consciousness as the knowing quality of the mind that experiences that *vedanā*. Both aspects are similarly impermanent and dependently arisen. The broadening of perspective introduced in this way fosters an inner distance toward *vedanā*. It leads to being considerably less prone to succumbing to its impact by reacting with desire or aversion. It is precisely through such clear understanding of the different dimensions of the experience of *vedanā* that ignorance diminishes, weakening the tendency for *vedanā* to stimulate the arising of various types of craving.

NOT SELF

A direct counterpart or complement to the doctrine of dependent arising is the teaching on the absence of a permanent self anywhere in subjective experience. In addition to the philosophical perspective of denying the existence of a permanent entity, from a practical viewpoint important dimensions of the same teaching are the countering of self-centered conceit and of a tendency to appropriation as "mine" through possessiveness and clinging. The three dimensions of the teaching on not self that emerge in this way are conveniently expressed in a standard phrase found repeatedly in the early discourses, according to which one should contemplate any aspect of subjective experience as not being "mine," not being what "I am," and not being a "self."[64] Contemplating in this way can target craving, conceit, and mistaken views in turn.

A proper appreciation of the teaching on not self as a meditative strategy requires keeping in mind that the absence of a permanent self does not imply that there is nothing at all. It only implies that everything, without exception, is changing and conditioned. The dependently arisen and impermanent flow of subjective experience by way of five aggregates (bodily form, *vedanā*, perception, volitional formations, and consciousness) certainly is there. But this is just an impermanent and dependently arisen process, which is devoid of some sort of unchanging and self-sufficient essence or entity.

Similarly, targeting the notion "I am" for meditative scrutiny is not meant to imply that we are no longer allowed to use the word "I." Awakened ones can still use the first person singular pronoun and the discourses show the Buddha to have had no qualms about saying, for example, "I have backpain; I want to rest."[65] The task is only to become aware of the tendency toward selfing, the self-referentiality that is almost continuously present in the background of unawakened experience.

In the same vein, classifying things as "not mine" does not imply that we can no longer own anything at all. Even monastics, in spite of having renounced worldly possessions, own things like their bowls or robes, etc. After having reached full awakening, the knowledge that a certain bowl or robe is "mine" will still be possible and even meaningful for them. What the meditative strategy puts into question is only the sense of possessiveness, the *clinging* to things as "mine." This clinging makes it difficult, if not impossible, to let go of what has been appropriated in this way with attachment, which inevitably leads to sorrow and affliction if anything happens to those things. A broken bowl and a torn robe can only upset those who own them with clinging.

How these different avenues of insight into not self can be related to *vedanā* emerges from another passage in the same *Mahānidāna-sutta* (DN 15). Although this part of the discourse is somewhat complex and requires some effort to be understood, it can yield powerful support for insight meditation.

The relevant passage begins with the Buddha (here referred to as the Tathāgata) declaring that there are three ways in which the notion of a self could be related to *vedanā*, followed by taking up each of these options for closer scrutiny in order to show their unconvincing nature. In the *Dīrgha-āgama* parallel to the *Mahānidāna-sutta*, the first option taken up for such closer scrutiny identifies the self with *vedanā*:[66]

Ānanda, as to a person who has the view of self, declaring that '*vedanā* is the self,' one should tell that person: 'The Tathāgata has taught three [types of] *vedanā*: pleasant *vedanā*, painful *vedanā*, and neutral *vedanā*.'

At the time when there is pleasant *vedanā*, there is no painful *vedanā* or neutral *vedanā*. At the time when there is painful *vedanā*, there is no pleasant *vedanā* or neutral *vedanā*. At the time when there is neutral *vedanā*, there is no painful *vedanā* or pleasant *vedanā*.

Ānanda, the reason for this is that pleasant *vedanā* arises in dependence on pleasant contact. If pleasant contact ceases, the *vedanā* also ceases. Ānanda, painful *vedanā* arises in dependence on painful contact. If painful contact ceases, the *vedanā* also ceases. [Ānanda,] neutral *vedanā* arises in dependence on neutral contact. If neutral contact ceases, the *vedanā* also ceases.

Ānanda, it is like rubbing together two firesticks to kindle a fire.[67] Putting each of them in a different place, there will consequently be no fire. This is also like that: Because pleasant *vedanā* arises in dependence on pleasant contact, if pleasant contact ceases, that *vedanā* also ceases completely. Because painful *vedanā* arises in dependence on painful contact, if painful contact ceases, that *vedanā* also ceases completely. Because neutral *vedanā* arises in dependence on neutral contact, if neutral contact ceases, that *vedanā* also ceases completely.

Ānanda, these three *vedanā*s are conditioned and impermanent, being born of conditions, and they are of a nature to end, of a nature to cease, of a nature to become decayed. They do not belong to a self and there is no self in them. With right knowledge one should contemplate them as they really are. Ānanda, as to the person who has the view of self, by taking *vedanā* to be the self, that is consequently to be rejected.

The parallel versions agree in highlighting the mutually exclusive nature of the three *vedanā*s, which is what counters identifying a particular *vedanā* as a self. The corresponding examination in the *Mahānidāna-sutta* directly targets the main problem resulting from the fact that three different types of *vedanā* exist. Which of these three is supposed to be the self?[68] A parallel in the *Madhyama-āgama* proceeds similarly:[69]

You have three [types of] *vedanā*: pleasant *vedanā*, painful *vedanā*, and neutral *vedanā*. Of these three [types of] *vedanā*, which *vedanā* do you view as the self?

The question posed in this way clarifies the main problem with the notion that equates *vedanā* with the self (the alternative idea that the self experiences all those different *vedanā*s will be taken up later). Which of these three mutually exclusive *vedanā*s is supposed to be the self? If one of them were to be identified as the self, what happens when one of the others manifests?

The passage translated above from the *Dīrgha-āgama* discourse stands alone in providing additional support for establishing this mutually exclusive nature. It achieves this by directing attention to contact as the condition for *vedanā*. This can conveniently be related back to an earlier part of the *Mahānidāna-sutta* and its parallels, which in the context of a detailed examination of dependent arising highlights the role of contact as what precedes *vedanā* and serves as the condition for its arising.

Contacts by way of any of the six sense doors occur one after the other. It is not the case that contacts by way of different sense doors occur simultaneously. Although this may sometimes seem to be the case from a subjective perspective, closer inspection shows that what really happens is a quick succession of different contacts. Each type of contact in turn conditions the type of *vedanā* that arises in dependence on it. This form of presentation clarifies why the three types of *vedanā* are seen as mutually exclusive.

The *Dīrgha-āgama* version also offers an illustration of the conditioned dependence of *vedanā* on contact with the help of a simile of two fire sticks, a simile not found in the parallel versions. The fire sticks will only produce fire if they are rubbed against each other. Just as anyone in the ancient Indian setting would have known from personal experience that the rubbing of fire sticks provides the indispensable condition for making a fire, in the same way contact should be seen as providing the necessary condition for the arising of *vedanā*. It follows that, with the cessation of contact, the corresponding *vedanā* ceases. Although the simile of the two fire sticks is not found in the *Mahānidāna-sutta*, it does occur in other Pāli discourses and their parallels.[70]

Having in this way established the mutually exclusive nature of the three types of *vedanā*, the parallel versions continue by pointing out that *vedanā* is impermanent and of a nature to cease. Since positing a self in the ancient Indian setting implied positing a permanent and inherently blissful entity, it follows that *vedanā* cannot be identified as such a self. Bhikkhu Bodhi (1984/1995: 35) clarifies the underlying reasoning:

> If feeling is self, whatever attributes belong to feeling also belong to self and whatever happens to feeling also happens to self. Since feeling is impermanent,

conditioned, dependently arisen, and subject to destruction, it would follow that the same pertains to self. This is a conclusion the theorist could not accept, as it contradicts his conception of self as permanent, unconditioned, independent, and indestructible; yet his initial thesis forces it upon him. Further, all feeling ceases and disappears, so if one identifies a particular feeling as self, with the ceasing of that feeling one would have to assert that self has disappeared—for the theorist an unthinkable situation, as it would leave him without the self he is seeking to establish.

Exploring possible practice applications, the idea of identifying *vedanā* as a self can go beyond explicitly formulated views. In fact, whereas the view of self is left behind with stream-entry, selfing and conceit are only abandoned once full awakening has been reached. Hence the matter broached above is not yet settled once we no longer uphold explicit views of an eternal self. This in turn means that the same teaching can also have a bearing on tendencies of the untrained mind that are more subtle than the proposing of philosophical standpoints based on positing a permanent self.

A practical example would be the case of an excruciating pain in some part of the body. The tendency of the untrained mind is to become completely drawn into and absorbed in the pain, to the extent of fully identifying with the pain. The pain has become so intense that its experience captures the entire range of awareness such that it is no longer possible to discern anything else but the pain.

Here mindfulness can offer a cure for the tendency to become overwhelmed by the pain. A first step could simply be to make a conscious effort to direct attention to parts of the body that are not in pain right now. If, for example, the back is hurting terribly, what about the soles of the feet? The feet? The lower legs? The upper legs? By gradually introducing recognition of areas of the body that are not directly impacted by the pain, awareness broadens, and the pain no longer captivates the whole of the attentional field. After all, it is just a particularly strong *vedanā*.

In case the pain is of the type that affects the whole body, an approach would be to inquire if other possible diseases are also there. Take the case of strong fever that affects the whole body. What about toothache? Are the bones also broken? Stomach cramps? It turns out that there is quite a range of possible afflictions that are not present. Noticing which particular illnesses are right now absent can have a similar effect of preventing that the pain captivates the whole of the field of attention.

In each case, the idea is to find ways of lessening the identification with the pain, of diminishing the tendency to equate oneself with the experience of that particular *vedanā* and become completely engulfed in it. In one way or another, there will always be aspects of subjective experience that need not be dominated by that particular pain. Moreover, any *vedanā* will change; none will last forever. It is all just a process. No need to make it into more than it actually is, and in particular no need to identify with it.

Returning to the exposition in the *Mahānidāna-sutta* and its parallels, after having dismissed the notion that *vedanā* could be identified as a self, the parallels continue with the possibility of instead positing a relationship of the self to *vedanā*. This presumably intends to save the belief in a self from being contradicted by the mutually exclusive nature of the different *vedanā*s.

According to the *Dīrgha-āgama* version, someone holding this view would express it as follows: "*vedanā* is not the self; the self is the one who feels."[71] In the *Madhyama-āgama* parallel, this position takes the similar form of someone who "does not view *vedanā* as the self, but views the self as being able to feel, it being the nature of the self to be able to feel."[72]

The chief problem with this proposition is the impermanent nature of *vedanā*s. The experiencing of something that is impermanent must also be a changing phenomenon itself, otherwise it would be forever frozen in the condition of knowing just one thing. If the ability to know is considered a permanent entity, its very permanency implies that it could no longer know change. The very knowing of change implies that the knowing itself has also changed. In other words, to turn a function (here the function of feeling *vedanā*s) into a permanent entity makes it become dysfunctional.

The only possibility to avoid that the proposed permanent entity is not affected by the changing nature of experiences is to posit it as something completely apart from the function of experiencing. As a result of such a move, however, this entity would become unable to feel *vedanā*s (a position to be examined below). But the ability to feel impermanent *vedanā*s must itself be amenable to change in order to be able to perform its function.

A practical application of the above could take the form of directing attention to the tendency to appropriate and own *vedanā*. This can also be applied to the case of physical pain, of course, where a shift from "my pain" to just "pain" and from "my body" being afflicted to just "the body" being afflicted can make a world of difference. Since pain has already been taken up above, however, it seems appropriate to explore also the case of pleasant *vedanā*. After all, it is particularly with agreeable experiences that the tendency to appropriation can manifest strongly, by way of wanting to own the pleasure and keep it forever. To counter such a tendency, it can be helpful to make it a continuous habit to share any joy or happiness with others. Such sharing is not confined to material sharing, although that is of course a prominent way of implementing the basic attitude. A traditional practice that exemplifies the basic attitude is sharing one's merits. In this or any other way, the task is simply to counter any tendency to appropriate what is liked by right away sharing it with others.

Returning once again to the exposition in the *Mahānidāna-sutta* and its parallels, yet another possibility of positing a self would be to completely dissociate this self from *vedanā*, in the sense of proposing that the two are just unrelated to each other and the proposed self does not feel any *vedanā*. The *Madhyama-āgama* version presents this as involving the view that "the self is without feeling."[73] Yet, this attempt also fails to provide a satisfactory solution. Bhikkhu Bodhi (1984/1995: 36) explains:

> Fundamental to the notion of selfhood is an inherent capacity for self-affirmation; as the autonomous subject of experience, self should be able to affirm its own being and identity to itself without need for external referents. Yet, the theorist is forced to admit that, with the cessation of feeling, in the complete absence of feeling, the idea 'I am this' could not be conceived. The assumed self can only identify itself as 'this,' e.g. 'I am the experiencer of feeling,' by reference to its psychophysical adjuncts. If these are removed, all points of reference for self to conceive its identity are removed and it then becomes a conceptual cipher ... The question clinches the point that the supposed self, being incapable of identifying itself without

reference to its adjuncts, becomes totally dependent upon them for its identity—a strange predicament for an autonomous self to get into.

In other words, the notion of a self is intrinsically bound up with experience. A self that is dissociated from experience, being unable to feel or be conscious, becomes a meaningless position. Precisely because it has been completely dissociated from actual experience, it becomes somewhat irrelevant to understanding and dealing with actual experience.

From a practical perspective, developing a meditative approach related to this position could take the form of noting the extent to which *vedanā* is integral to experience. For such exploration, neutral *vedanā* would be of particular importance, as its contemplation shows that the absence of pleasure and pain is not the absence of *vedanā*. Once the all-pervasive and continuous role of *vedanā* in experience has been fully appreciated in this way, it becomes clear that any type of experience necessarily will involve some *vedanā* or the other.

An exception to this rule, in the sense of being a type of experience where *vedanā* is absent, is the realization of Nibbāna. Yet, this is at the same time the type of experience where any basis for the notion of a self completely disappears. In a way, selfing and conceit are intimately bound up with *vedanā*. Their cessation comes through the direct experience of the ceasing of *vedanā* that occurs when the entire chain of dependent arising ceases.

Looking back on the positions surveyed in the *Mahānidāna-sutta* and its parallels, a natural starting point for contemplation of not self, besides the more specific practical dimensions already surveyed above, is mindful contemplation of the impermanent nature of *vedanā*. In the absence of a proper understanding, the experience of *vedanā* can easily become interwoven with a subjective sense of an enduring 'I' or 'me' as the one who feels. The tendency for this subjective sense to manifest needs to be noticed alongside awareness of the constant change of *vedanā* from one feeling tone to another. The impermanent nature of *vedanā*, evident in this way, clearly shows that this sense of a permanent 'I' at the center of experience cannot be identified with *vedanās*, because they keep changing all the time. It also undermines the idea of a permanent agent that feels *vedanā*, because *vedanās* that change from one type to another inevitably involve a variety of experiences. Hence, their knowing needs to be something changing as well. Nor does it make sense to posit a permanent experiencer completely apart from the felt experience of change.

The potential of contemplation of the impermanent nature of *vedanās* to lead to insight into not self can be strengthened by catching within the purview of attention the sense of an 'I' lurking at the background of the meditative experience. With the groundwork laid by previous reflection along the lines of the above discourse passages, the implications of not self can emerge in an intuitive way that involves only a minimal amount of conceptual input. All it takes is applying the explorations proposed in the *Mahānidāna-sutta* and its parallels to actual practice in such a way that understanding deepens and freedom from attachment grows.

THE GENESIS OF VIEWS

The next passage in a way builds on the foundational insight into the dependently arisen nature of *vedanā* by way of pinpointing its conditional relationship to the genesis of views. The relevant passage occurs in the *Dīrgha-āgama* parallel to the *Brahmajāla-sutta*, the Discourse on Brahmā's Net (DN 1). Whereas in the *Dīgha-nikāya* collection the *Brahmajāla-sutta* occurs before the *Mahānidāna-sutta*, in the *Dīrgha-āgama* extant in Chinese translation the corresponding parallels occur in the opposite sequence, with the parallel to the *Mahānidāna-sutta* (DĀ 12) occurring before the parallel to the *Brahmajāla-sutta* (DĀ 21).

The *Brahmajāla-sutta* and its parallels survey different ways in which views can arise. Contrary to a popular interpretation, this survey is not an attempt to provide an exhaustive account of views in ancient India.[74] Instead, its concern is what causes the arising of views. The sixty-two cases taken up for examination are in fact not sixty-two distinct views, but much rather sixty-two grounds (*vatthu*) for the arising of views. The first four grounds surveyed, for example, all lead to proposing the single view of eternalism. In this way, the concerns of the *Brahmajāla-sutta* and its parallels are to expose the genesis of views, the view-forming process, rather than debate non-Buddhist doctrinal propositions.

Of particular significance here is that a considerable part of the exposition takes up views that arise, in one way or another, out of misinterpretations of meditative experiences. Bhikkhu Bodhi (1978/1992: 6) notes:

The fact that a great number [of the views], perhaps the majority, have their source in the experience of meditative attainments has significant implications for our understanding of the genetic process behind the fabrication of views. It suffices to caution us against the hasty generalization that speculative views take rise through preference for theorization over the more arduous task of practice. As our sutta shows, many of these views make their appearance only at the end of a prolonged course of meditation ... For these views the very basis of their formulation is a higher experience rather than the absence of one.

The warning that emerges in this way on potential misinterpretations of meditative experiences comes together with a pointer toward what can solve the dilemma of latching on to views. This solution is none other than contemplation of the true nature of *vedanās*, as these are the key element leading to attachment to views and opinions.[75] The affective investment in dogmatic adherence to personal beliefs relies on the power of *vedanās* to captivate the mind. The bedrock of the required antidote lies in the clear recognition of the impermanent nature of all *vedanās*. The relevant passage highlights such clear recognition, together with its results, in the following manner:[76]

[The Buddha] knows the arising of *vedanās*, their cessation, their gratification, their disadvantage, and the release from them. By way of his unbiased vision, he has been liberated without remainder, for which reason he is called a Tathāgata.

In the early discourses in general, a term used regularly by the Buddha to refer to himself is "Tathāgata."

Although the term can be translated in different ways, a likely prominent sense in the usage reflected in the early discourses would be "the Thus-gone One."[77] The present passage clarifies that the nuance of transcendence inherent in the term Tathāgata can be directly related to vedanās. It is by way of fully understanding vedanās that the Buddha became liberated without remainder and deserves to be reckoned a Tathāgata. Needless to say, the same type of full understanding can lead to the full awakening of an arahant. Hence, there is indeed good reason to dedicate oneself fully to meditation aimed at penetrative insight into vedanās.

Such insight requires combining a clear recognition of the impermanent nature of vedanās with knowing the gratification that vedanās, especially pleasant ones, can provide. This gratification comes inexorably intertwined with a disadvantage, which is precisely grounded in the impermanent nature of vedanās. The more we attach and cling to vedanās at those times when they provide gratification, the more we suffer when that gratification comes to an end. For this reason, the release can be found in the absence of attachment and the giving up of clinging.

This basic pattern can in turn conveniently be applied to any dogmatically held view, especially by clearly discerning the sense of gratification that clinging to the view can provide. The gratification experienced becomes all too evident if we have trained in the recognition of vedanās. Such recognition enables witnessing the degree to which vedanās tends to color apparently well-reasoned thoughts and reflections, how the initial input provided by vedanā in a way sets the course of the mind. When the basic predisposition provided by vedanā has not been clearly noticed, the mind only too easily gets carried away by subsequent attempts to rationalize likes and dislikes, which eventually become firmly entrenched views and strongly held opinions. Noting the beginning stages of this process through close attention to *vedanās* can help to step out of the pull and push created by the oppositional forces of subjective likes and dislikes. Such stepping out is not only relevant to dogmatic views and rigid opinions. It can also unfold its potential in relation to the interpretation of our own meditative experiences. What counts, in the end, is finding release from the bondage of bias so easily created by *vedanās*.

In practical terms, this requires bringing contemplation of the affective tone of *vedanās* to bear on those moments when our ideas and opinions are being challenged, when someone else forcefully proposes the precise opposite of what we think is correct. The task is not to remain silent and pretend indifference. Often a response or clarification is indeed called for, but this should come with clear awareness of our own affective involvement through mindful contemplation of *vedanās*. In fact, responses or clarifications perform their task much better if they come from a balanced mind that is able to step out of the affective pull of identification with personal views and opinions.

ATTACHMENT AND JOY

With the next topic, my exploration shifts from the collections of long discourses to those of medium length, one of which was already mentioned above as an additional parallel to the *Mahānidāna-sutta*. The passage under discussion now occurs in the *Madhyama-āgama* parallel to the *Saḷāyatanavibhaṅga-sutta* (MN 137). In the context of several perspectives on sense experience, the two parallel discourses take up the topic of different types of joy (as well as of sadness and equanimity) that can arise in relation to each of the six senses.

The chief distinction here is between types of joy that are related to attachment and those that are related to its absence, a topic that already came up earlier in relation to a *Saṃyukta-āgama* discourse in the context of a division of *vedanās* into thirty-six types (see p. 41). The *Saḷāyatanavibhaṅga-sutta* expresses the basically same contrast with the terms "based on the household" (*gehasita*) and "based on renunciation" (*nekkhammasita*). The terminology employed here should not be taken too literally as being about lay life in contrast to monastic life. In fact, the Chinese and Tibetan parallels express the same distinction in terms of contrasting "attachment" to its absence. The point is simply to introduce an ethical distinction in relation to experiences that have the same pleasant affective tone. The relevant exposition in the *Madhyama-āgama* parallel to the *Saḷāyatanavibhaṅga-sutta* presents the case of visual experience in this way:[78]

> Having seen a form with the eye, joy arises. One should know this to be of two types; it could depend on attachment or it could depend on dispassion.

What is joy based on attachment? The eye comes to know forms that are conducive to joy and the mind reflects on them, craves for those forms, and experiences happiness conjoined with desire. One desires to obtain those [forms] which one has not obtained, and on having recollected those which one has already obtained, joy arises. Joy of this type is reckoned joy based on attachment.

What is joy based on dispassion? One understands that forms are impermanent, changing, [of a nature to] disappear, fade away, cease, and subside; that all forms, both formerly and in the present, are impermanent, unsatisfactory, and of a nature to cease. Having recollected this, joy arises. Joy of this type is reckoned joy based on dispassion.

The *Madhyama-āgama* version continues by applying the same exposition to the other senses of the ears, nose, tongue, body, and mind. A minor difference in presentation is that the Pāli parallel first works through all six senses for one type of joy and only then turns to the other type of joy in relation to the same six senses.

From a practical perspective, the passage can be taken to highlight a crucial point. Chasing after pleasant experiences through the senses just leads to increasing attachment. Once again, the key to counter the tendency toward succumbing to attachment is simply directing mindfulness to the impermanent nature of *vedanā*. If impermanence is clearly seen, the path of dispassion opens up and the danger of attachment diminishes. Hence, in terms of practical implementation, this particular teaching mainly calls for contemplating the impermanent nature of all *vedanās*.

Notably, implementing this mode of practice does not require avoiding all types of joy. It is not the case that dispassion equals having only bland or even unpleasant experiences. Instead, staying free from attachment can in turn serve as a source of joy.

COMMENDABLE JOY

The indication that some types of joy are commendable, already evident in the passage taken up above, can be explored further with the help of the *Kīṭāgiri-sutta* (MN 70) and its *Madhyama-āgama* parallel. The narrative setting of the discourse shows a group of monastics unwilling to follow the Buddha's injunction to restrain their food intake by not eating at night. After rebuking them for their obstinate behavior, the Buddha explained that his instructions were based on his own knowledge and insight into the potential repercussions of pleasant *vedanās*. The relevant part in the *Madhyama-āgama* discourse proceeds as follows:[79]

> If I had not known as it really is, had not seen, had not understood, had not grasped, had not rightly and completely realized that there can be pleasant *vedanās* that increase [bad and] unwholesome states and decrease wholesome states, it would not be proper for me to teach the abandoning of such pleasant *vedanās*.
>
> If I had not known as it really is, had not seen, had not understood, had not grasped, had not rightly and completely realized that there can be pleasant *vedanās* that decrease bad and unwholesome states and increase wholesome states, it would not be proper for me to teach the cultivation of such pleasant *vedanās*.

Both versions apply the same explanation to unpleasant and neutral *vedanās*. This passage confirms the conclusion drawn above, in that progress of insight is not just about avoiding all that is pleasant and giving oneself as hard a time as possible. Of course, some pleasures need to be left behind, in clear recognition of their potential to keep us in bondage. These are the pleasant *vedanās* that increase unwholesome states. But other pleasant *vedanās* instead increase wholesome states. These could include the joy of maintaining moral conduct, of sharing one's possessions with others, of deepening concentration, and above all the joy of insight and letting go.

Keeping in mind that the crucial distinction is not between pleasure and pain, but between *vedanās* that foster what is wholesome and those that stimulate what is unwholesome, can serve as a guiding principle for conduct and practice. Adopting this guiding principle is a way of directly walking in the footsteps of the Buddha himself. It actualizes a key insight he developed during his own quest for awakening.[80]

In short, and presented in a way that directly relates to the topic of *vedanā*, during his quest for awakening the Buddha-to-be had cultivated the higher two of the immaterial spheres, states of profound concentration that are characterized by neutral *vedanās*. Then he engaged in ascetic practices, which involve self-inflicted pain. The inability of both approaches to lead him to liberation made him reflect and realize that there is no need to be afraid of happiness as such.[81] There are pleasant *vedanās* not related to sensuality that are wholesome and which for this reason can contribute to progress to awakening.

The decisive insight that the ethical dimension of a particular experience is more important than its affective tone found further corroboration in the three higher knowledges the Buddha attained in the night of his awakening, where recollection of his own past lives and witnessing the passing away and rearising of sentient beings enabled a direct witnessing of the repercussions of wholesome and unwholesome actions. Notably, the description of recollection of his own past lives explicitly mentions the pleasure and pain experienced in various past lives, thereby providing a direct relationship to the topic of *vedanā*. All of this then prepared the ground for the destruction of the unwholesome influxes (*āsavā*) in his mind, which was the third and decisive higher knowledge attained during the night of his awakening.

In sum, then, insight into the nature of *vedanā*s and the overarching importance of their ethical quality instead of their affective tone can be seen as a crucial aspect in the Buddha's own quest for liberation and can serve as a guiding principle for anyone who wishes to progress to awakening.

COUNTERPARTS

The three types of *vedanā* can be related to a series of counterparts that step by step lead up to Nibbāna, thereby in a way exemplifying the awakening potential of contemplation of *vedanā*s. An exposition on this topic is part of the *Cūḷavedalla-sutta* (MN 44), which has an arahant nun as its speaker. The discourse covers a range of topics, one of which is the listing of counterparts. Here is the relevant part from the *Madhyama-āgama* parallel (which comes with elisions of repeated reports of the delighted reaction of the questioner, in order to allow the actual exposition to stand out more clearly).[82]

"Noble one, what is the counterpart to pleasant *vedanā*?" The nun Delight in Dhamma replied:[83] "The counterpart to pleasant *vedanā* is unpleasant *vedanā*." ...

"Noble one, what is the counterpart to unpleasant *vedanā*?" The nun Delight in Dhamma replied: "The counterpart to unpleasant *vedanā* is pleasant *vedanā*." ...

"Noble one, what is the counterpart to pleasant *vedanā* and unpleasant *vedanā*?" The nun Delight in Dhamma replied: "The counterpart to pleasant *vedanā* and unpleasant *vedanā* is neutral *vedanā*." ...

"Noble one, what is the counterpart to neutral *vedanā*?" The nun Delight in Dhamma replied: "The counterpart to neutral *vedanā* is ignorance." ...

"Noble one, what is the counterpart to ignorance?" The nun Delight in Dhamma replied: "The counterpart to ignorance is knowledge." ...

"Noble one, what is the counterpart to knowledge?" The nun Delight in Dhamma replied: "The counterpart to knowledge is Nibbāna."

The *Cūḷavedalla-sutta* proceeds with some differences. It does not present neutral *vedanā* as the counterpart to both pleasant and unpleasant ones. Whereas in this respect the *Cūḷavedalla-sutta* is shorter, it has an additional counterpart before coming to Nibbāna. This is liberation (*vimutti*) as the counterpart to knowledge. A reference to liberation fits well with the previous reference to knowledge (*vijjā*), the two terms occurring regularly together elsewhere in the discourses. An example is the *Ānāpānasati-sutta*, which offers instructions on developing the four establishments of mindfulness (*satipaṭṭhāna*) based on the breath in such a way as to lead to the cultivation of the awakening factors (*bojjhaṅga*), which in turn culminates in knowledge and liberation.[84]

Alongside such differences, however, the parallel versions agree on leading an exploration of counterparts from the different types of *vedanā* to the final goal. This is the point at which the series stops, as Nibbāna no longer has any counterpart, be this in the form of a direct opposite or in the form of a complementary item.

The whole series of counterparts (taking into account also those not found in all versions) can be seen to provide a succinct trajectory from the ordinary experience of *vedanā* to the final goal of Nibbāna. This trajectory begins by juxtaposing pleasant and unpleasant *vedanā*, revealing that the heights of pleasure come at the cost of pain, simply because the one does not exist without the other. Both taken together then have their complement in neutral *vedanā*, an area in the spectrum of felt experience between the poles of pleasure and pain, defined by the fact that it is neither really pleasant nor really unpleasant. The exact compass of this area needs to be staked out by each practitioner individually, in the sense of deciding what precisely is the range of *vedanās* in subjective experience that is no longer pleasant and not yet really unpleasant.

From having in this way surveyed the whole compass of the affective tonality of *vedanā*, the presentation shifts to overall conditions of the mind. Here, neutral *vedanā* has its counterpart in ignorance. In fact, neutral *vedanā* is usually quite literally "ignored." Even if noted, neutral *vedanā* tends to trigger the "ignorant" quest for something more entertaining, at least in the untrained mind. Neutral *vedanā* is seen as just too boring, hence the wish to replace it with something more exciting as soon as possible.

Ignorance (*avijjā*) as the root cause of all defilements and the starting point of the dependent arising of *dukkha* has knowledge (*vijjā*) as its opposite, which in actual practice involves, among other things, making an effort to recognize with mindfulness the presence of neutral *vedanā* as well as to develop insight into what all *vedanās* have in common: the nature to arise and cease.

Such knowledge has a clear instrumental purpose, which is to bring about liberation. The liberation to be gained in this way can be related back to the contrast between pleasant and unpleasant *vedanā*, taken up at the beginning of the series of counterparts. It all boils down to gaining increasing degrees of liberation from the tendency of the untrained mind to be in bondage to pleasure and pain, by reacting to them with defilements. This is the overarching purpose of the teachings and their practical implementation; hence Nibbāna forms the concluding and culminating point of the series of counterparts.

Understood in this way, the series of counterparts can be taken as a basic overview of progress in insight in contemplation of *vedanās*. Adopting the above passage as such a basic orientating point has the advantage of having an accomplished woman as its speaker. In a world otherwise densely populated by males, it can be a heartening inspiration to turn to teachings given by a female saint, such as the arahant nun who presented this powerful series of counterparts (which, be it noted, is just a portion of a powerful discourse given by her on various aspects of the teachings).

CONTEMPLATION OF *VEDANĀ*

The final passage to be taken up stems from the last of the four Chinese *Āgamas*, the *Ekottarika-āgama*. The relevant discourse is one of the two Chinese *Āgama* parallels to the *Satipaṭṭhāna-sutta* (MN 10); the other parallel is found in the *Madhyama-āgama*. The passage translated below concerns contemplation of *vedanās*, which serves as the second of the four establishments of mindfulness:[85]

> How do monastics [in regard to] *vedanās* contemplate *vedanās* internally? Here, at the time of having a pleasant *vedanā*, monastics are aware of it and know of themselves: 'We are having a pleasant *vedanā*.' At the time of having an unpleasant *vedanā*, they are aware of it and know of themselves: 'We are having an unpleasant *vedanā*.' At the time of having a neutral *vedanā*, they are aware of it and know of themselves: 'We are having a neutral *vedanā*.'
>
> At the time of having a worldly pleasant *vedanā*, they are in turn aware of it and know of themselves: 'We are having a worldly pleasant *vedanā*.' At the time of having a worldly unpleasant *vedanā*, they are in turn aware of it and know of themselves: 'We are having a worldly unpleasant *vedanā*.' At the time of having a worldly neutral *vedanā*, they are also aware of it and know of themselves: 'We are having a worldly neutral *vedanā*.'
>
> At the time of having an unworldly pleasant *vedanā*, they are in turn aware of it and know of themselves: 'We are having an unworldly pleasant *vedanā*.' At the time of having an unworldly unpleasant *vedanā*, they are also aware of it and know of themselves: 'We are having an unworldly unpleasant *vedanā*.' At the time

of having an unworldly neutral *vedanā*, they are also aware of it and know of themselves: 'We are having an unworldly neutral *vedanā*.'

In this way, [in regard to *vedanās*] monastics contemplate *vedanās* internally.

Again, at the time when monastics have a pleasant *vedanā*, then at that time they do not have an unpleasant *vedanā*; at that time they are aware and know of themselves: 'We are experiencing a pleasant *vedanā*.' At the time when they have an unpleasant *vedanā*, at that time they do not have a pleasant *vedanā*; they are aware and know of themselves: 'We are experiencing an unpleasant *vedanā*.' At the time when they have a neutral *vedanā*, at that time there is no pain or pleasure; they are aware and know of themselves: 'We are experiencing a neutral *vedanā*.'

They [contemplate] the nature of arising, experiencing joy in themselves, they also contemplate their nature of ceasing, and they then contemplate their nature of arising and ceasing.

Further, they are able to know and able to see that these are *vedanās* that manifest here and now, giving attention to their origination. Not depending on anything, they experience joy in themselves, not arousing mundane perceptions.

Herein they are also not agitated, and because of not being agitated they in turn attain Nibbāna, knowing as it really is that 'birth and death have been extinguished, the holy life has been established, what had to be done has been done, there is no more experiencing of [another] existence.'

In this way monastics contemplate *vedanās* internally by themselves, discarding distracted thoughts and being without worry and sorrow; they contemplate *vedanās* externally by themselves, and they contemplate *vedanās* internally and externally, discarding distracted thoughts and being without worry and sorrow. In this way monastics contemplate *vedanās* internally and externally.

In agreement with its parallels, the above *Ekottarikaāgama* version directs attention first of all to the three distinct affective tones of *vedanā*. This is in line with a recurrent emphasis in the various passages surveyed above. The rationale behind this injunction appears to lie in the potential of bringing mindfulness to bear on the initial affective input by *vedanā*. The problem here is that this often enough takes place below the threshold of our awareness. This is not to say that this initial input has no impact, which indeed it has and at times to a remarkable degree. But the way this impact influences evaluations and reactions happens at a level of the mind that is usually not consciously noticed. The experience of *vedanā* is an integral part of daily life and the tendency to react with liking toward what is pleasant and with dislike toward what is unpleasant is deeply ingrained in the mind. It takes quite some effort in training in mindfulness for this habitual pattern of reacting to *vedanā* to be recognized.

In actual practice, the impact of this habitual reactivity is best explored by keeping in view the condition of the mind alongside recognition of the particular *vedanā* that has arisen. This could well be why the instructions in all three discourse versions proceed from recognition of the three affective tones to an application of the distinction between worldly and unworldly occurrences of each.

On following the indications provided in the discourse discussed above (see p. 39), this additionally distinction would be related to the relevant underlying tendencies. Worldly pleasant *vedanās* of the type related to sensual indulgence need to be distinguished from unworldly pleasant *vedanās*, which are apart from sensuality. The same holds for unpleasant and neutral *vedanās*, where those related to aversion and delusion need to be set apart from unpleasant and neutral *vedanās* that do not activate the respective underlying tendencies. Undertaking contemplation of *vedanās* in this way strengthens the ability to monitor with mindfulness any possible mental reactivity to the experience of *vedanā* and ensure that the mind stays within the realm of what is wholesome.

A major difference between the three versions manifests next, as the above extract stands alone in drawing attention to the mutually exclusive nature of the three types of *vedanā*. Although this part could well be a later addition, in a way it only makes explicit what would be implicit in the other versions. It is not possible, strictly speaking, to experience pleasure and pain, for example, right at the same moment. Although from a subjective perspective this might at times appear to be the case, close inspection brings to light that there is much rather a mixture of quickly alternating *vedanās*, some of which are pleasant and others unpleasant.

Whatever the type of *vedanā* may be, the key instruction for the cultivation of liberating insight is to contemplate their arising and ceasing, that is, their impermanent nature.[86] A qualification of such practice, made only in the above-translated *Ekottarika-āgama* discourse, is that such contemplation leads to "experiencing joy" in oneself. Although not mentioned in the *Satipaṭṭhāna-sutta* or its

Madhyama-āgama parallel, actual practice will soon be able to confirm that witnessing with mindfulness the impermanent nature of all that is felt is indeed productive of wholesome joy.

The *Ekottarika-āgama* version offers further elaboration when it describes how practitioners, "not depending on anything, they experience joy in themselves, not arousing mundane perceptions." The very abandonment of mundane perceptions and the deepening understanding of impermanence are what can indeed lead to becoming more and more independent of anything, which results in experiencing increasing degrees of unworldly joy within.

Such practice, as the discourse explicitly indicates, leads to leaving behind agitation and to progressing to the realization of Nibbāna. Even though the parallel versions do not explicitly mention Nibbāna in their descriptions of contemplation of *vedanā*s, both do present the same as the result to be expected from *satipaṭṭhāna* meditation in general. For this reason, the indication in the *Ekottarika-āgama* discourse can be considered to draw out explicitly what is implicit in its parallels.

The final part of the above instruction brings up the topic of contemplating *vedanā*s internally or externally.[87] An early and important work of the Theravāda *Abhidhamma* collection, the *Vibhaṅga*, conveys the impression that external contemplation of *vedanā*s refers to those experienced by others.[88] On this understanding, such external practice would no longer be a matter of direct experience. Instead, it would require some degree of drawing inferences, at least for the majority of practitioners who are not able to avail themselves of telepathic abilities. The tone of voice, facial expression, and body language of others can provide quite evident indications as to whether they are experiencing pleasant, unpleasant, or neutral *vedanā*. Observing how *vedanā* impacts and influences others could in this way complement internal observation of the same basic mechanisms within oneself. Although this offers a viable understanding that I personally find quite convincing, there are various alternative interpretations of contemplation undertaken externally.[89] Whichever interpretation we may prefer to adopt, the required task can be summed up as requiring a contemplation of *vedanā* as comprehensively as possible.

A final point to be explored concerns the very existence, in the *Satipaṭṭhāna-sutta* and its parallels, of contemplation of *vedanā*s as a *satipaṭṭhāna* in its own right. Given that the third *satipaṭṭhāna* covers the whole of the mind (*citta*), why should another *satipaṭṭhāna* just be dedicated to one aspect of the mind, namely *vedanā*?[90] If various aspects of the mind each deserve a *satipaṭṭhāna* of their own, then why not also take up perception (*saññā*), for example?

The same question presents itself again in a different form when considering the themes under which discourses are arranged in the *Saṃyutta-nikāya* (and in its counterpart, the *Saṃyukta-āgama*). In addition to a section on the whole set of five aggregates (SN 22) and on the whole set of the four *satipaṭṭhāna*s (SN 47), another whole section is dedicated to the topic of *vedanā* (SN 36). Precisely this section is the source of many of the discourses translated above, which provide such rich perspectives on the practice of the second *satipaṭṭhāna*, contemplation of *vedanā*s. No comparable section exists on the topic of "perception" (*saññā*) or even on "the mind" (*citta*);[91] although a chapter on this topic exists in the *Dhammapada*.[92]

In a way, the excerpts from the discourses on *vedanā* translated above provide an answer to this question. Simply said, it must be the immense potential of contemplation of *vedanās* that has earned it such a position of eminence. A key dimension of this potential lies in the position of *vedanā* at a crucial junction in the dependent arising of *dukkha*, where the presence of mindfulness can exert a decisive influence on the manifestation of craving. It is precisely at this junction that mindfulness of the affective push provided by *vedanā* is crucial in order to avoid that this push triggers craving and clinging.

Due to the role of the affective push of *vedanā* in the process of experience, mindful observation of its influence can have a considerable impact at an incipient stage in the formation of thoughts and reactions, making it possible to recognize and deal with unwholesomeness when it is just emerging and has not yet acquired much force.

In addition, the actual contemplation of *vedanās* offers such a palpable and direct experience of impermanence, based on which the other two characteristics of *dukkha* and not self naturally fall into place. In all these interrelated ways, contemplation of *vedanās* deserves to be reckoned as a particularly powerful approach for the cultivation of liberating insight.

Conclusion

A metaphor that can offer considerable help when facing *vedanā*s describes bubbles arising on the surface of a pond during rain. Different *vedanā*s are just like such bubbles; they arise and soon enough burst and disappear. The contact that stimulates those *vedanā*s could be happening at any of the six sense doors. This offers another avenue for deepening insight, namely by way of recognizing which particular sense door has given rise to *vedanā*, together with clearly noting what all *vedanā*s have in common: they arise and soon enough disappear again.

Instead of being at the beck and call of the three types of *vedanā*, in the sense of just being at the mercy of the push and pull of its affective quality and vainly hoping that it will stay (if pleasant) or disappear (if unpleasant), attention can turn toward discerning the impermanent nature of the experience of *vedanā*. If the particular affective tone of *vedanā* requires being attended to, then this can take the form of contemplating pleasant types in such a way as to overcome the underlying tendency to passion, unpleasant ones to remove the tendency to aversion, and neutral ones to emerge from the tendency to ignorance. Contemplating the three types of *vedanā* in this way serves as an implementation of right view, the guiding factor of the noble eightfold path.

Pain as one of the three *vedanā*s can be like a bottomless abyss, hence there is a dire need to avoid the additional dart of mental suffering when confronted with physical affliction. The possibility of avoiding the additional dart shows that even pain need not result in suffering. Suffering is the reaction of an untrained mind; it is not a qualification applicable to all conditioned phenomena. These are *dukkha* in the sense of being unsatisfactory, as without exception they are unable to yield true and lasting satisfaction.

The "gratification" to be found in *vedanā* comes inexorably intertwined with the "disadvantage" that, sooner or later, this gratification is going to end. For this reason, stepping out of craving provides the "release" from the predicament of being enslaved by *vedanā*. In actual practice, this can take the form of identifying contact as the key condition for a particular *vedanā* to arise, followed by ascertaining if there is some form of craving that keeps fueling such arising. If that is the case, the gratification experienced through this *vedanā* needs to be placed into context by turning awareness to the unavoidable disadvantage inherent in its impermanent nature. Framing insight into the impermanent nature of *vedanā*s in this way can have a remarkable liberating potential and lead to true inner renunciation.

The distinction of *vedanā*s into worldly and unworldly types appears to introduce an awareness of the quality of the mind within which a particular *vedanā* occurs: Is the present state of mind wholesome or unwholesome? Is it free of the activation of the underlying tendencies or does it much rather trigger them? This type of inquiry into the ethical quality of the mind, reflecting an overarching concern with the presence or absence of attachment, is at the same time the converging point of other analyses of *vedanā*s into various types, which can even involve discerning up to one hundred and eight types. Whether we prefer to stay simple or have a propensity for employing detailed schemes of analysis, it all boils down to one single question: Does the *vedanā* that has manifested now increase *dukkha* or decrease it?

As long as practice evolves along this basic trajectory, it will lead in the direction of freedom. From this perspective, then, the question of karma is of secondary importance. Of course, some *vedanās* arise as the fruition of what had formerly been done, no doubt. A corresponding reflection can help establish patience when having to face such fruition. But the overall task is not to expiate former deeds. Instead, the task is cultivating liberating insight with any *vedanā*, be it arisen due to former karma or due to any other cause. In other words, exploring the conditionality of *vedanā* need not reach out into the distant past, but can more fruitfully be employed to discern present conditions.

In the case of physical pain, attention to its dependence on the body can be of considerable assistance in arousing patience and avoiding an activation of the underlying tendency to aversion. Besides serving to face physical pain, mindful contemplation of *vedanās* can also offer assistance in relation to partaking of food by learning to know one's measure. In addition to the mundane benefit of bodily health and avoidance of an overweight condition, penetrative insight into the *vedanās* related to taste can even further progress to awakening.

In the series of specific conditions that lead to the manifestation of *dukkha*, *vedanā* is the crucial point at which craving can, but does not have to manifest. At this juncture, the presence of mindfulness can make a world of difference. This can take the form of shining the light of awareness and understanding on a dimension of experience where ignorance usually holds sway, which is by way of immediate reaction to the affective quality of *vedanā* with desire and aversion.

Another approach to exploring the conditionality of *vedanā* relates to its position among the factors that make up "name" in name-and-form. From a practical viewpoint, the reciprocal conditioning relationship between name-and-form and consciousness can be taken as the basis for a broadening of the field of meditative experience. This can take place by including in the purview of awareness the knowing of what is taking place. In addition to being mindful of *vedanās*, for example, such a form of practice can involve being also mindful of consciousness as the dimension of the mind that knows *vedanās*. Besides offering an intriguing perspective on the conditionality of *vedanā*, contemplating in this way also has the practical advantage of making it easier to notice when the mind is about to get distracted, thereby facilitating the swift deployment of countermeasures to ensure continuity of practice.

Contemplation of the changing nature of *vedanā* provides a firm foundation for the growth of insight into not self. Such insight proceeds through successive layers of the mind's ingrained habit of self-referentiality. Based on relinquishing the explicit view of affirming the existence of a permanent self, increasingly subtler traces of conceit and possessiveness need to be successively overcome until with full awakening all selfing in any form will be removed for good. For insight into not self to unfold its full potential, it can be helpful to dedicate time and attention to clearly discerning the sense of self-referentiality that tends to stand at the background of unawakened experience. The more selfing is clearly recognized, the easier it becomes to remove and transcend it.

The problem of identification manifests also in relation to views and opinions, where the affective input provided by *vedanā* can easily lead to strong reactions and dogmatic insistence. Here the task of mindfulness is to foster a clear recognition of any affective investment in one's own views and opinions, in order to be able to remain balanced when these are being challenged.

Contemplation of the impermanence of *vedanās*, as the key to avoid attachment and clinging, does not entail having to avoid all types of joy. Appreciating this requires a clear distinction of joy into those types that are related to attachment and those free from it. The joy of deep insight, the joy of letting go, and the joy of increasing purification of the mind are all commendable; they offer powerful support for the path to freedom. A guiding principle for conduct and practice can be the understanding that the crucial distinction to be made is not between pleasure and pain, but between *vedanās* that foster what is wholesome and those that rather trigger what is unwholesome. Inspiration for adopting this guiding principle can be gained by keeping in mind that this actualizes an outcome of the Buddha's own realization, gained during his quest for awakening. In this way, an orientation toward the realization of Nibbāna can serve as the chief reference point for contemplation of *vedanās*, which, based on the simple distinction into three affective types, leads to such realization via the gradual removal of ignorance.

The instructions on formal mindfulness practice as the second of the four *satipaṭṭhānas* bring the various insight perspectives on *vedanā* together by conveying that, from a practical perspective, the chief tasks are to recognize the affective tone of any *vedanā* (pleasant/unpleasant/neutral) and to discern its ethical quality (worldly/unworldly), in the sense of the mental context within which it has arisen. Remaining aware of its impermanent nature opens up the path to freedom.

ABBREVIATIONS

AN	*Aṅguttara-nikāya*
CBETA	Chinese Buddhist Electronic Text Association
D	Derge edition
DĀ	*Dīrgha-āgama* (T 1)
Dhp	*Dhammapada*
DN	*Dīgha-nikāya*
EĀ	*Ekottarika-āgama* (T 125)
MĀ	*Madhyama-āgama* (T 26)
MN	*Majjhima-nikāya*
P	Peking edition
Ps	*Papañcasūdanī* (commentary on MN)
SĀ	*Saṃyukta-āgama* (T 99)
SĀ²	*Saṃyukta-āgama* (T 100)
SN	*Saṃyutta-nikāya*
Sn	*Sutta-nipāta*
T	Taishō edition (CBETA)
Up	*Abhidharmakośopāyikā-ṭīkā*
Vibh	*Vibhaṅga*

Bibliography

Akanuma Chizen 1929/1990: *The Comparative Catalogue of Chinese Āgamas & Pāli Nikāyas*, Delhi: Sri Satguru.

Anālayo 2003: *Satipaṭṭhāna, the Direct Path to Realization*, Birmingham: Windhorse Publications.

Anālayo, Bhikkhu 2009: "Views and the Tathāgata – A Comparative Study and Translation of the Brahmajāla in the Chinese Dīrgha-āgama," in *Buddhist and Pali Studies in Honour of the Venerable Professor Kakkapalliye Anuruddha*, K.L. Dhammajoti et al. (ed.), 183–234, Hong Kong: Centre of Buddhist Studies, University of Hong Kong.

Anālayo, Bhikkhu 2011a: "Chos sbyin gyi mdo, Bhikṣuṇī Dharmadinnā Proves Her Wisdom," *Chung-Hwa Buddhist Journal*, 24: 3–33.

Anālayo, Bhikkhu 2011b: *A Comparative Study of the Majjhima-nikāya*, Taipei: Dharma Drum Publishing Corporation.

Anālayo, Bhikkhu 2013a. "On the Five Aggregates (2) – A Translation of Saṃyukta-āgama Discourses 256 to 272," *Dharma Drum Journal of Buddhist Studies*, 12: 1–69.

Anālayo, Bhikkhu 2013b: *Perspectives on Satipaṭṭhāna*, Cambridge: Windhorse Publications.

Anālayo, Bhikkhu 2014: *The Dawn of Abhidharma*, Hamburg: Hamburg University Press.

Anālayo, Bhikkhu 2015: *Compassion and Emptiness in Early Buddhist Meditation*, Cambridge: Windhorse Publications.

Anālayo, Bhikkhu 2016: *Mindfully Facing Disease and Death, Compassionate Advice from Early Buddhist Texts*, Cambridge: Windhorse Publications.

Anālayo, Bhikkhu 2017a: *A Meditator's Life of the Buddha, Based on the Early Discourses,* Cambridge: Windhorse Publications.

Anālayo, Bhikkhu 2017b: "Some Renditions of the Term Tathāgata in the Chinese *Āgamas*," *Annual Report of the International Research Institute for Advanced Buddhology at Soka University,* 20: 11–21.

Anālayo, Bhikkhu 2018a: "Overeating and Mindfulness in Ancient India, *Mindfulness,* 9.5: 1648–1654.

Anālayo, Bhikkhu 2018b: *Rebirth in Early Buddhism and Current Research,* Boston: Wisdom Publications.

Anālayo, Bhikkhu 2018c: "Why Be Mindful of Feelings?" *Contemporary Buddhism, Special Issue: Knowing How it Feels: The Definition, Practice, and Psychology of vedanā,* 19.1: 47–53.

Anālayo, Bhikkhu 2019a: "Comparing the Tibetan and Chinese Parallels to the Cūḷavedalla-sutta," in *Investigating Principles: International Aspects of Buddhist Culture,* L. Shravak and S. Roy (ed.), 1–36, Hong Kong: The Buddha-Dharma Centre of Hong Kong.

Anālayo, Bhikkhu 2019b: *Mindfulness of Breathing: A Practice Guide and Translations,* Cambridge: Windhorse Publications.

Anālayo, Bhikkhu 2020a: "Attention and Mindfulness," *Mindfulness,* 11.5: 1131–1138.

Anālayo, Bhikkhu 2020b: "Consciousness and Dependent Arising," *Insight Journal,* 46: 55–63.

Anālayo, Bhikkhu 2020c: "Dependent Arising," *Insight Journal,* 46: 1–8.

Anālayo, Bhikkhu 2020d: "External Mindfulness," *Mindfulness,* 11.7: 1632–1646.

Anālayo, Bhikkhu 2020e: "Ichimura Shohei, The Canonical Book of the Buddha's Lengthy Discourses," *Indian International Journal of Buddhist Studies*, 21: 159–170.

Anālayo, Bhikkhu 2020f: *Mindfulness in Early Buddhism, Characteristics and Functions*, Cambridge: Windhorse Publications.

Anālayo, Bhikkhu 2020g: "Once Again on External Mindfulness," *Mindfulness*, 11.11: 2651–2657.

Anālayo, Bhikkhu 2021: "Dependent Arising and Interdependence," *Mindfulness*, 12: 1094–1102.

Anālayo, Bhikkhu and R. S. Bucknell 2020: *The Madhyama Āgama (Middle-Length Discourses), Volume II*, Moraga, California: Bukkyō Dendō Kyōkai America.

Bechert, Heinz and Klaus Wille 1989: *Sanskrithandschriften aus den Turfanfunden, Teil 6*, Stuttgart: Franz Steiner.

Bechert, Heinz and Klaus Wille 2000: *Sanskrithandschriften aus den Turfanfunden, Teil 8*, Stuttgart: Franz Steiner.

Bingenheimer, Marcus, Bh. Anālayo, and R. S. Bucknell 2013: *The Madhyama Āgama (Middle Length Discourses), Volume I*, Berkeley: Bukkyō Dendō Kyōkai America.

Bodhi, Bhikkhu 1978/1992: *The All-Embracing Net of Views, The Brahmajāla Sutta and its Commentaries, Translated from the Pali*, Kandy: Buddhist Publication Society.

Bodhi, Bhikkhu 1984/1995: *The Great Discourse on Causation, The Mahānidāna Sutta and its Commentaries, Translated from the Pali*, Kandy: Buddhist Publication Society.

Bodhi, Bhikkhu 2000: *The Connected Discourses of the Buddha, A New Translation of the Saṃyutta Nikāya*, Boston: Wisdom Publications.

Bodhi, Bhikkhu 2012: *The Numerical Discourses of the Buddha, A Translation of the Aṅguttara Nikāya*, Boston: Wisdom Publications.

Choong Mun-keat 2000: *The Fundamental Teachings of Early Buddhism, A Comparative Study Based on the Sūtrāṅga portion of the Pāli Saṃyutta-Nikāya and the Chinese Saṃyuktāgama*, Wiesbaden: Otto Harrassowitz.

Chung Jin-il 2008: *A Survey of the Sanskrit Fragments Corresponding to the Chinese Saṃyuktāgama*, Tokyo: Sankibo.

Chung Jin-il 2019: "A Sanskrit Fragment Corresponding to Sūtra 481 of the Za-ahan-jing," *Hokkaido Journal of Indian Philosophy and Buddhism*, 3: 65–91.

Dhammadinnā, Sāmaṇerī 2013: "A Translation of the Quotation in Śamathadeva's Abhidharmakośopāyikā-ṭīkā Parallel to the Chinese Saṃyukta-āgama Discourse 265," *Dharma Drum Journal of Buddhist Studies*, 12: 71–84.

Dhammadinnā, Bhikkhunī 2019: "Discourses on Feeling Tones (*vedanā*), Quoted in Śamathadeva's Abhidhar-makośopāyikā-ṭīkā", *The Indian International Journal of Buddhist Studies*, 20: 159–184.

Faust-Koschinger, Regina 1999: *Das Bahuvedanīyasutta im Textvergleich*, MA thesis, Mainz: Johannes Gutenberg-Universität.

Ichimura Shohei 2016: *The Canonical Book of the Buddha's Lengthy Discourses, Volume II*, Moraga, California: Bukkyō Dendō Kyōkai America.

Jurewicz, Joanna 2000: "Playing with Fire: The Pratītyasamutpāda from the Perspective of Vedic Thought," *Journal of the Pali Text Society*, 26: 77–103.

Ñāṇamoli, Bhikkhu 1995/2005: *The Middle Length Discourses of the Buddha, A Translation of the Majjhima Nikāya*, Bhikkhu Bodhi (ed.), Boston: Wisdom Publications.

Sander, Lore 1987: *Nachträge zu ,Kleinere Sanskrit-Texte Heft III-V'*, Wiesbaden: Franz Steiner.

Soma Thera 1941/1981: *The Way of Mindfulness, The Satipaṭṭhāna Sutta Commentary*, Kandy: Buddhist Publication Society.

Tripāṭhī, Chandrabhāl 1962: *Fünfundzwanzig Sūtras des Nidānasaṃyukta*, Berlin: Akademie Verlag.

Waldschmidt, Ernst 1932: *Bruchstücke Buddhistischer Sūtras aus dem zentralasiatischen Sanskritkanon, Herausgegeben und im Zusammenhang mit ihren Parallelversionen bearbeitet*, Leipzig: F.A. Brockhaus.

Walshe, Maurice 1987: *Thus Have I Heard; The Long Discourses of the Buddha*, London: Wisdom Publications.

Weller, Friedrich 1934: *Brahmajālasūtra, Tibetischer und Mongolischer Text*, Leipzig: Otto Harrassowitz.

Wille, Klaus 2017: *Sanskrithandschriften aus den Turfanfunden Teil 11*, Stuttgart: Franz Steiner.

Ye Shaoyong 2009: "Or. 15009/201–250," in *Buddhist Manuscripts from Central Asia, The British Library Sanskrit Fragments, Volume II*, S. Karashima and K. Wille (ed.), 227–257, Tokyo: International Research Institute for Advanced Buddhology, Soka University.

NOTES

1 Here and elsewhere, I translate only extracts, leaving aside the opening and concluding sections of the respective discourse.

2 SĀ 265 at T II 68c8 (translated by Anālayo 2013a: 35), parallel to SN 22.95 at SN III 141,5 (translated by Bodhi 2000: 951), T 105 at T I 501a15, T 106 at T I 501c21, Up 4084 at D 4094 *ju* 239a6 or P 5595 *tu* 273a8 (translated by Dhammadinnā 2013: 75).

3 SN 22.95 adds that this happens during autumn; see also Dhammadinnā 2013: 75n8.

4 SN 22.95 and T 106 do not have the comparisons to a disease, etc., and also do not mention impermanence and *dukkha*, topics taken up in T 105 and Up 4084.

5 SĀ 304 at T II 87a4, parallel to MN 148 at MN III 281,28 (translated by Ñāṇamoli 1995/2005: 1130), and Up 3059 at D 4094 *ju* 159b2 or P 5595 *tu* 184a7.

6 SĀ 304 at T II 87a11.

7 SĀ 372 at T II 102a25, parallel to SN 12.12 at SN II 13,26 (translated by Bodhi 2000: 541), and Up 9028 at D 4094 *nyu* 87a6 or P 5595 *thu* 134a5.

8 Ps I 275,4: *ko vediyatī ti*? (translated by Soma 1941/1981: 108), whose formulation corresponds to SN 12.12 at SN II 13,25: *ko nu kho, bhante, vediyatī ti*? (with the difference that, since in SN 12.12 this question is addressed to the Buddha, the formulation comes with the respectful address "venerable sir").

9 *Saṃyukta-āgama* discourses in this section that do not have a Pāli parallel will only be mentioned briefly but not be translated.

10 SĀ 466 at T II 119a15, parallel to SN 36.10 at SN IV 215,1 (translated by Bodhi 2000: 1270).

11 The simile also occurs as an illustration of the same dependency of *vedanā* on contact in SN 12.62 (and MN 140), in which cases it is also found in the parallels; see below note 70. This makes it possible that its occurrence in the present context is a case of a transfer of this simile, something

that could easily have happened in the course of oral transmission.

12 SĀ 467 at T II 119a26, parallel to SN 36.5 at SN IV 207,5 (translated by Bodhi 2000: 1263) a Sanskrit fragment in Ye 2009: 231, and Up 6012 at D 4094 *nyu* 7a3 or P 5595 *thu* 39a5 (translated by Dhammadinnā 2019: 161).

13 SĀ 468 at T II 119b15, parallel to SN 36.3 at SN IV 205,8 (translated by Bodhi 2000: 1261), and the same Sanskrit fragment parallel in Ye 2009: 231 that also has preserved a counterpart to the preceding SĀ 467.

14 The translation is based on an emendation by deleting a reference to "contemplating pleasant *vedanā*." Since such a reference is not found for the other two types of *vedanā*, it seems probable that its occurrence here is due to an accidental copying of this phrase from the preceding discourse.

15 Translations of the verses can be found in Choong 2000: 119f and Anālayo 2013b: 140f.

16 SĀ 469 at T II 119c8, parallel to SN 36.4 at SN IV 206,7 (translated by Bodhi 2000: 1262), the same Sanskrit fragment parallel in Ye 2009: 231 that also has preserved a counterpart to the preceding discourses SĀ 467 and SĀ 468, and SHT XII 6740, Wille 2017: 251.

17 The translation is based on an emendation by deleting a reference to "the great ocean." This seems to be out of place here, presumably a copying error influenced by the beginning of the discourse, which is indeed about an abyss in the great ocean.

18 SĀ 469 at T II 119c24 and SN 36.4 at SN IV 207,1.

19 SĀ 470 at T II 119c29 (translated by Anālayo 2016: 29), parallel to SN 36.6 at SN IV 207,24 (translated by Bodhi 2000: 1263).

20 The translation is based on emending a reference to "underlying tendency" to read "*vedanā*".

21 The translation "gratification" is based on an emendation suggested in the CBETA edition.

22 In SN 36.6 at SN IV 210,6 the Buddha sums up that this is the difference between the worldling and the noble disciple.

23 SN 36.6 at SN IV 208,11.

24 SN 36.6 at SN IV 208,20.

25 SĀ 471 at T II 120b16 (translated by Anālayo 2013b: 132), parallel to SN 36.12 at SN IV 218,6 (translated by Bodhi 2000: 1272).

26 The absence of such verses is what marks the difference between SN 36.12 and SN 36.13, the latter of which only has the prose portion. In general, a comparatively high percentage of discourses in the *Vedanā-saṃyutta* is accompanied by verse, compared to other *saṃyutta*s found outside of the *Sagātha-vagga*. Several of these other *saṃyutta*s cover quite important doctrinal or practice-related topics, such as causality, the five aggregates, the six sense spheres, the eightfold path, the awakening factors, the four establishments of mindfulness, etc. Perhaps this characteristic of the *Vedanā-saṃyutta* could be taken to convey the importance accorded to the topic it covers, as a verse that summarizes the gist of a discourse is more easily remembered even by those who are not trained in the recitation of the texts. Such a verse can thus conveniently serve as a reference point and inspiration for actual contemplation of *vedanā*s. Moreover, a verse can speak to us more on an intuitive level than a prose exposition. Such an approach is quite apt for the case of *vedanā*s, whose contemplation can foster an intuitive sense for what is presently happening in the mind.

27 SĀ 472 at T II 120c9 (translated by Anālayo 2013b: 133), parallel to SN 36.14 at SN IV 219,9 (translated by Bodhi 2000: 1273).

28 Anālayo 2013b: 117f.

29 SĀ 474 at T II 121a23 (extracts of which have been translated by Choong 2000: 109 and 126), parallel to SN 36.11 at SN IV 216,13 (translated by Bodhi 2000: 1270) and Up 6010 at D 4094 *nyu* 6a3 or P 5595 *thu* 37b6 (translated by Dhammadinnā 2019: 164). Dhammadinnā 2019: 163n12 lists SN 36.15–16 as parallels to SĀ 474. Although these two discourses have Ānanda as their speaker and take up the gradual cessation/ tranquilization of formations, they do not set out on the central question of why all *vedanā*s are *dukkha*. This makes it seem to me preferable to consider SN 36.11 as the proper parallel to SĀ 474, even though the Pāli version just has an unnamed monk rather than Ānanda as its protagonist.

Regarding the preceding discourse SĀ 473, Akanuma 1929/1990: 55 and Chung 2008: 134 list SN 36.1 as a parallel. Yet, SN 36.1 only lists the three types of *vedanā*, whereas SĀ 473 takes up the same question as SĀ 474, namely why all *vedanās* have been qualified as *dukkha* when they are of three distinct types. The difference between SĀ 473 and SN 36.1 seems to be too pronounced to consider them to be parallels. On this reasoning, then, SĀ 473 would be without a Pāli parallel and for this reason has not been translated here.

30 The translation is based on two emendations; the original speaks of the gradual "tranquilization" of all "*vedanās*," apparently a copying error; for the latter see Dhammadinnā 2019: 165n21.

31 SĀ 475 at T II 121b29, parallel to SN 36.24 at SN IV 233,13 (translated by Bodhi 2000: 1281). SĀ 475 actually introduces the text as a pre-awakening reflection of a previous Buddha, known in the Pāli tradition under the name of Vipassin. The discourse ends by indicating that the same reflection should be repeated for other Buddhas who lived subsequent to Vipassin, up to and including the Buddha Gotama himself.

32 SĀ 476 at T II 121c14 and its parallel SN 36.23 at SN IV 232,27 (translated by Bodhi 2000: 1281), feature an unnamed monastic as the questioner, whereas in SĀ 477 at T II 121c29 and SN 36.15 at SN V 219,28 the questions are posed by Ānanda and in SN 36.17 at SN IV 221,23 and SN 36.25 at SN IV 234,15 by a group of monastics. SĀ 478 at T II 122a3 and SN 36.18 at SN IV 223,1 then report the Buddha asking a group of monastics about their opinion on these matters, to which they reply by requesting him to expound it; in SN 36.16 at SN V 221,7 the same takes place with the Buddha asking Ānanda instead.

33 SĀ 480 at T II 122b4, parallel to SN 36.26 at SN IV 234,31 (translated by Bodhi 2000: 1282, referred to as SN 36.27), as well as to the next two discourses SN 36.27 and SN 36.28.

34 The next two discourses in the *Saṃyukta-āgama* have Pāli parallels located outside of the collection on the topic of *vedanā*. Their presentation does indeed not appear to be as directly relevant to insight into *vedanā* as the preceding discourses in the collection. The first of these two discourses

is SĀ 481 at T II 122b13, parallel to SN 45.11 at SN V 12,9 (translated by Bodhi 2000: 1531; see also SN 45.12, which differs in reporting that the Buddha had gone on retreat for three months instead of half a month), and Sanskrit fragments in Chung 2019. The second discourse is SĀ 482 at T II 122c24, parallel to AN 5.176 at AN III 206,22 (translated by Bodhi 2012: 789) and Up 8020 at D 4094 *nyu* 72b7 or P 5595 *thu* 117b4 (translated by Dhammadinnā 2019: 170).

35 SĀ 483 at T II 123b4, parallel to SN 36.29 at SN IV 235,27 (translated by Bodhi 2000: 1284, referred to as SN 36.31).

36 SĀ 484 at T II 123c16, parallel to AN 5.170 at AN III 202,28 (translated by Bodhi 2012: 785).

37 MN 119 at MN III 92,25 (translated by Ñāṇamoli 1995/2005: 953) and its parallel MĀ 81 at T I 555b18 (translated in Anālayo and Bucknell 2020: 103).

38 On the different identities of the protagonists see Anālayo 2011b: 335f.

39 MN 59 at MN I 397,36 (translated by Ñāṇamoli 1995/2005: 503) and SN 36.19 at SN IV 224,28 (translated by Bodhi 2000: 1275).

40 SN 36.22 at SN IV 231,30 (translated by Bodhi 2000: 1280).

41 SĀ 485 at T II 124a5 (for a survey of the list see Choong 2000: 113), with its Tibetan parallel in Up 6007 at D 4094 *nyu* 5a2 or P 5595 *thu* 36b1 (translated by Dhammadinnā 2019: 175).

42 Faust-Koschinger 1999: 33 understands this third type to refer to *vedanās* that are not bound to forms ("das Gefühl, das nicht durch die Bindung an Formen (entsteht).") However, the negation qualifies forms (and not the bondage), corresponding to the standard way of designating "formless" or "immaterial" experiences or realms.

43 The Tibetan parallel Up 6007 at D 4094 *nyu* 5a6 or P 5595 *thu* 36b8 (translated by Dhammadinnā 2019: 176) relates this last category to the absence of the influxes, *zag pa med pa*.

44 See Anālayo 2011b: 337 in relation to the present instance and Anālayo 2014 on the emergence of the Abhidhamma.

45 SĀ 485 at T II 124b9, parallel to MN 59 at MN I 400,11 and SN 36.19 at SN IV 228,8; see also SHT VIII 1884V, Bechert and Wille 2000: 73, and SHT XII 6684, Wille 2017: 180. The translation is

based on the assumption that a reference to "realizing with the body" intends to convey the sense of "directly realizing;" see Anālayo 2011b: 379n203.

46 The final four discourses in this part of the *Saṃyukta-āgama*, SĀ 486 to SĀ 489, do not have a Pāli parallel.

47 SĀ 977 at T II 253a6, parallel to SN 36.21 at SN IV 230,19 (translated by Bodhi 2000: 1279); see also SĀ² 211 at T II 452b27.

48 SĀ 1028 at T II 268c17 (translated by Anālayo 2016: 162), parallel to SN 36.7 at SN IV 212,3 (translated by Bodhi 2000: 1267).

49 The rendering adopted here is only tentative, as the formulation in the original is rather cryptic.

50 The translation is based on an emendation by deleting a reference to "and," on the assumption that this would be a copying error influenced by the earlier reference to "the body and" in the description of the contemplation of impermanence, etc.

51 See in more detail Anālayo 2019b: 100–119 and 2013b: 219–226.

52 SĀ 1150 at T II 306c3 (translated by Anālayo 2020f: 177) parallel to SN 3.13 at SN I 81,21 (translated by Bodhi 2000: 176) and SĀ² 73 at T II 400a1 (translated by Anālayo 2018a: 1649).

53 See Anālayo 2018a and 2020f: 175–181.

54 MN 91 at MN II 138,26 (translated by Ñāṇamoli 1995/2005: 747) and a parallel in MĀ 161 at T I 687b5; see also T 76 at T I 884b1.

55 SĀ 373 at T II 102c3, parallel to SN 12.63 at SN II 99,8 (translated by Bodhi 2000: 598).

56 MN 28 at MN I 190,37 (translated by Ñāṇamoli 1995/2005: 284), which has a Chinese *Āgama* parallel in MĀ 30 at T I 467a9 (translated in Bingenheimer et al. 2013: 233).

57 See also Anālayo 2021.

58 See Jurewicz 2000 and Anālayo 2020c.

59 SN 12.2 at SN II 3,34 (translated by Bodhi 2000: 535), with a parallel in EĀ 49.5 at T II 797b28 (translated by Anālayo 2020a: 1132; see also Anālayo 2018b: 10n21).

60 DĀ 13 at T I 61b19, parallel to DN 15 at DN II 56,31 (translated by Walshe 1987: 223), where the corresponding part occurs at an earlier junction of the discourse. A similar statement can be found in the other parallels to DN 15 that are extant in Chinese: MĀ 97 at T I 580a1 (translated in Anālayo and Bucknell 2020: 214), T 14 at T I 243c2, and T 52 at T I 845b11. The present passage in DĀ 13 has already been translated by Ichimura 2016: 32. Unfortunately, his translations are often unreliable and at times even seriously misleading; see in more detail Anālayo 2020e. In the present case, he translates the part after name-and-form in this way: "the sixfold sense operation depends on sense contact; sense contact depends on sensation and sensation depends on thirstlike craving; thirstlike craving depends on grasping and grasping depends on the will-to-becoming; the will-to-becoming depends on birth and birth depends on old age, death, sorrow, lamentation, suffering and agony." In this way, besides adding terms not found in the original ("operation," "thirstlike," "will-to") and omitting others (the arising of the great mass of *dukkha*), he inverts the conditional relationship between the individual links. As a result, *vedanā* is made to depend on craving or else birth to depend on old age and death. This patently fails to make sense.

61 See also Anālayo 2020b.

62 SN 12.67 at SN II 114,17 (translated by Bodhi 2000: 608), with a Sanskrit fragment parallel in Tripāṭhī 1962: 110, a Chinese parallel in SĀ 288 at T II 81b5, and a Tibetan parallel in Up 8005 at D 4094 *nyu* 70a5 or P 5595 *thu* 114b2. SĀ 288 differs from the other versions by speaking of three bundles of reeds; see Anālayo 2015: 109n16.

63 On the latter see Anālayo 2018b: 12–17.

64 For example, MN 22 at MN I 136,6 (translated by Ñāṇamoli 1995/2005: 229), and its parallel MĀ 200 at T I 765c7.

65 Anālayo 2011b: 35n55.

66 DĀ 13 at T I 61c6, parallel to DN 15 at DN II 66,14 (translated by Walshe 1987: 227), in addition to which there are a few relevant Sanskrit fragments in Waldschmidt 1932: 9f (see also 56f), Sander 1987: 149f, and Bechert and Wille 1989: 41 and 60, Chinese discourse parallels in T 14 at T I 243c12, MĀ 97 at

T I 580a11 (translated in Anālayo and Bucknell 2020: 215), and T 52 at T I 845b29, and a parallel preserved in Tibetan in Up 4068 at D 4094 *ju* 231a7 or P 5595 *tu* 264a7.

67 The translation "rubbing" is based on adopting a variant reading; the original speaks instead of "accumulating."

68 DN 15 at DN II 66,15.

69 MĀ 97 at T I 580a12.

70 One such occurrence is MN 140 at MN III 242,31 (translated by Ñāṇamoli 1995/2005: 1091), with counterparts in the Chinese and Tibetan parallels MĀ 162 at T I 691b27, T 511 at T XIV 780c3, and Up 1041 at D 4094 *ju* 39a6 or D 5595 *tu* 42b6. Another occurrence is SN 12.62 at SN II 97,9 (translated by Bodhi 2000: 597), again found also in the Sanskrit and Chinese parallels Tripāṭhī 1962: 120 and SĀ 290 at T II 82a20. Another occurrence is SN 36.10 at SN IV 215,21 (translated by Bodhi 2000: 1270), but in this case the illustration does not occur in the parallel SĀ 466 at T II 119a11 (see above note 10). Yet another occurrence is in SN 48.39 at SN V 212,21 (translated by Bodhi 2000: 1683), of which no parallel is known.

71 DĀ 13 at T I 61c22.

72 MĀ 97 at T I 580a9.

73 MĀ 97 at T I 580a11 (the presentation of this view in DĀ 13 appears to have suffered from a textual corruption and for this reason is not taken up here).

74 See in more detail Anālayo 2009.

75 See in more detail Anālayo 2003: 161.

76 DĀ 21 at T I 90b13, parallel to DN 1 at DN I 17,2 (translated by Walshe 1987: 75), T 21 at T I 266b4, T 1548 at T XXVIII 657a12, Weller 1934: 22,2, and Up 3050 at D 4094 *ju* 144b3 or P 5595 *tu* 166a6. The last two and T 21 just draw attention to impermanence, without bringing in the triad of gratification, disadvantage, and escape (corresponding to *assāda*, *ādīnava*, and *nissaraṇa* in Pāli).

77 See in more detail Anālayo 2017b.

78 MĀ 163 at T I 692c20, parallel to MN 137 at MN III 217,13 (translated by Ñāṇamoli 1995/2005: 1067) and Up 3069 at D 4094 *ju* 166a5 or P 5595 *tu* 191b8.

79 MĀ 195 at T I 750c27, parallel to MN 70 at MN I 475,28 (translated by Ñāṇamoli 1995/2005: 579).

80 See in more detail Anālayo 2017a: 74–76.

81 MN 36 at MN I 247,3 (translated by Ñāṇamoli 1995/2005: 340); on the parallels see Anālayo 2011b: 242f.

82 MĀ 210 at T I 789c22, parallel to MN 44 at MN I 304,8 (translated by Ñāṇamoli 1995/2005: 402) and Up 1005 at D 4094 *ju* 10b6 or P 5595 *tu* 12a1 (translated by Anālayo 2011a: 18); see also Anālayo 2019a.

83 The nun in MN 44 has the name Dhammadinnā instead, a name also reflected in the Tibetan parallel Up 1005 as *Chos sbyin*.

84 MN 118 at MN III 88,2 (translated by Ñāṇamoli 1995/2005: 948) and SĀ 810 at T II 208a21 (translated by Anālayo 2019b: 203).

85 EĀ 12.1 at T II 568b27 (translated by Anālayo 2013b: 290), parallel to MN 10 at MN I 59,11 (translated by Ñāṇamoli 1995/2005: 149; see also DN 22 at DN II 298,8, translated by Walshe 1987: 339) and MĀ 98 at T I 583c24 (translated by Anālayo 2013b: 277).

86 Contemplation of impermanence is not explicitly mentioned in MĀ 98 at T I 584a2.

87 The parallel MĀ 98 at T I 584a2 only mentions internal and external, not the combination of the two.

88 Vibh 196,7; a similar understanding can be seen in one of two alternative explanations of external contemplation of *vedanās* provided in the *Dharmaskandha*, T 1537 at T XXVI 477b5, a similarly important work in the Sarvāstivāda canonical Abhidharma collection.

89 See Anālayo 2003: 99–102 and for a detailed discussion Anālayo 2020d and 2020g.

90 For a more detailed discussion see Anālayo 2018c.

91 The *Citta-saṃyutta*, SN 41, concerns a lay disciple by the name of Citta. This collection is thus not on discourses related to the topic of *citta* as "the mind."

92 Dhp 33 to Dhp 43.

BHIKKHU ANĀLAYO was ordained in Sri Lanka where he completed his Ph.D. in Buddhist Studies. His thesis was published as *Satipaṭṭhāna: The Direct Path to Realization*. With over 400 academic publications, Ven. Anālayo is a leading scholar in research on Early Buddhism with a special interest in the topics of the position of women in Buddhism and Buddhist meditation. Recently retired from his position as a university professor in Germany, he is now a resident scholar at the Barre Center for Buddhist Studies in MA, USA, and spends most of his time in meditation.

ABOUT PARIYATTI

Pariyatti is dedicated to providing affordable access to authentic teachings of the Buddha about the Dhamma theory (*pariyatti*) and practice (*paṭipatti*) of Vipassana meditation. A 501(c)(3) nonprofit charitable organization since 2002, Pariyatti is sustained by contributions from individuals who appreciate and want to share the incalculable value of the Dhamma teachings. We invite you to visit www.pariyatti.org to learn about our programs, services, and ways to support publishing and other undertakings.

Pariyatti Publishing Imprints

Vipassana Research Publications (focus on Vipassana as taught by S.N. Goenka in the tradition of Sayagyi U Ba Khin)

BPS Pariyatti Editions (selected titles from the Buddhist Publication Society, copublished by Pariyatti in the Americas)

Pariyatti Digital Editions (audio and video titles, including discourses)

Pariyatti Press (classic titles returned to print and inspirational writing by contemporary authors)

Pariyatti enriches the world by

- disseminating the words of the Buddha,
- providing sustenance for the seeker's journey,
- illuminating the meditator's path.

Made in the USA
Middletown, DE
26 September 2022

11244763R00066